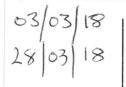

Servants' Stories

*For my grandmother, and all those
who toiled in domestic service*

Servants' Stories

Life Below Stairs in their Own Words 1800–1950

Michelle Higgs

PEN & SWORD HISTORY

First published in Great Britain in 2015 by
Pen & Sword History
an imprint of
Pen & Sword Books Ltd
47 Church Street
Barnsley
South Yorkshire
S70 2AS

ISBN 978 1 47382 224 5

A CIP catalogue record for this book is available from the British
Library

Typeset in Ehrhardt by
Mac Style Ltd, Bridlington, East Yorkshire
Printed and bound in the UK by CPI Group (UK) Ltd,
Croydon, CRO 4YY

Pen & Sword Books Ltd incorporates the imprints of Pen & Sword
Archaeology, Atlas, Aviation, Battleground, Discovery, Family
History, History, Maritime, Military, Naval, Politics, Railways, Select,
Transport, True Crime, and Fiction, Frontline Books, Leo Cooper,
Praetorian Press, Seaforth Publishing and Wharncliffe.

For a complete list of Pen & Sword titles please contact
PEN & SWORD BOOKS LIMITED
47 Church Street, Barnsley, South Yorkshire, S70 2AS, England
E-mail: enquiries@pen-and-sword.co.uk
Website: www.pen-and-sword.co.uk

Contents

Acknowledgements

It is impossible to write a book like this without the help of a great number of people. While working on *Servants' Stories*, I received assistance and advice in locating information and illustrations from a number of different sources.

For permission to reproduce extracts or images, I would like to express my gratitude to Jackie Brown of the British Library; Amy Sell of the British Newspaper Archive; the staff of Cambridgeshire Archives; Judy Davies of Codsall and Bilbrook Local History Society; the staff of the LSE Library; Peter Leigh of Pattingham Local History and Civic Society; Jane Mace, former editor of the SE1 People's History Project; Liz Stanley and Virago Press; Dr Mike Wood and the St Marylebone Society; Howard Dixon of Staffordshire and Stoke on Trent Archive Service; Sarah Williams of Tamworth Castle; Victoria Rimmer of the Walsall Local History Centre; and Kathryn Coles of the Workers' Educational Association.

Thanks are also due to Jen Newby, who first commissioned me for this project; to Eloise Hansen, my editor at Pen & Sword; to Helen Harwood, whose website alerted me to the existence of Amy Grace Rose's reminiscences; and to the staff of *Who Do You Think You Are?*, *Family Tree*, *Your Family Tree* and *Best of British* magazines, who publicised the fact that I was looking for servants' stories.

I would also like to thank the following people, who so generously shared their stories and research: Jenni Dobson, for the information about her grandmother Mary Doughty; Hilary Donaldson, for granting permission to publish extracts from an oral history interview given by her grandmother Cis Parker; Peter Few, for allowing me to reproduce the letter from his ancestor Louisa Mist; Angela Richardson, for the details about her family friend Doris Hailwood; and Anne Simmonds, for granting permission to publish extracts about her aunt, Marian Taylor from her unpublished biography, *The Singing Centenarian*.

Special thanks go to the ex-servants and families of former servants with whom I was privileged to correspond and interview during the writing of this book: Reverend David Dixon; John Ewen, Kathleen McNeill and Anne

Newton; Lindsay Hall; Pam Harris; Amy Jones; Daphne Jones and Colin Jones; Lily Kerry, Robert Kerry and Elizabeth Yule; and Rebecca Marsh.

Finally, I would like to thank my husband Carl for his continued support, and my family and friends for their encouragement during the writing of this book.

List of Illustrations

E very effort has been made to trace copyright holders of images included in this book. The publishers would be grateful for further information concerning any image for which we have been unable to trace a copyright holder.

Front cover image: Servants at Drayton Manor, Staffordshire, circa 1900. (With thanks to Tamworth Castle, ref. PH1247)

Introduction

My grandmother worked in domestic service in the late 1920s but, as she died when I was in my teens, I never had the chance to ask about her experiences. Researching and selecting the extracts for this book has given me a greater understanding of what her working life might have been like.

When I researched a previous book on domestic service, *Tracing Your Servant Ancestors* (Pen & Sword, 2012), most of the sources I came across represented the employers' point of view. This book tells the servants' side of the story, warts and all, and my grandmother would doubtless recognise many of the scenarios described. I have concentrated on the lesser-known stories of ordinary men and women who worked as servants in smaller homes for the middle and lower-middle classes, rather than the minority employed by the aristocracy on their country estates. In fact, in 1871 almost two-thirds of Britain's female domestic servants were classed as 'general servants' in homes employing one or two maids. However, the opposite was true for male servants, as they were mostly found in households keeping large numbers of domestic staff.

As a nation, we are fascinated by domestic service; the high viewing figures for *Downton Abbey* and visitor numbers to country houses represent ample proof of this. It may be the relationship between servant and employer, or the contrast between their very different lives, that intrigues us so much; perhaps it's the fact that domestic service so clearly represents the class divide; or we are simply nostalgic for lost Victorian and Edwardian values.

The stories in this book come from diaries, oral histories, autobiographies, letters, memoirs and newspaper reports; some are from sources now out of print, while others have never been published before. While reading these accounts, it must be borne in mind that it is impossible to generalise about the servant experience, since the nature of domestic service varied remarkably between employers. However, long hours, very hard work and an acutely felt loss of freedom are common themes in most of the stories reproduced here.

The period 1800–1950 saw huge changes in the roles of domestic servants, as well as the living conditions they could expect and their status in society. The 21 servants' stories in this book encompass this timespan and they are arranged in chronological order of the year each individual first went into service. Original spellings and punctuation have been retained to preserve the integrity of the extracts. The servants' stories appear alongside more general chapters about the nature of domestic service and the ways in which it altered during this period – from going into service and the growing 'servant problem' in the Victorian era through to Edwardian domestic service and the impact of war.

Even today, memories of domestic service evoke strong emotions in former servants: of pride in having served a kind employer well; of anger at being treated like another species; of despair after feeling completely and utterly alone; and of gratitude towards an employer who encouraged them to pursue further education.

These narratives do not feature fictional characters; they are honest accounts of real experiences told by real people and they deserve to be heard. Above all, stories of domestic service are human stories of hopes and dreams, of duty and personal sacrifice, and of determination and dignity.

Part I

1800–1850

Going into Service

HOUSEMAID WANTED. An active and industrious HOUSEMAID between 25 and 30 years of age, who can have an unexceptionable character from her last situation, in which she must have lived at least 12 months, is WANTED immediately. Apply at 246, Regent Street between 6 and 7 in the evening.

(*The Times*, 4 May 1847)

For much of the nineteenth century, when a working-class girl approached school-leaving age, her rite of passage into domestic service began. There was little alternative employment for the majority of young British women, especially in rural areas, except if they lived outside cities or industrial regions where mills and factories offered other forms of unskilled work. In 1851, there were almost one million domestic servants in Britain – 905,000 women and 134,000 men. This figure was only dwarfed by the number of people employed in agriculture (more than 1.5 million).

Going into service was far less common for boys, since they had access to many more opportunities to learn a skilled trade, usually via an apprenticeship. Yet, boys who lived near a country estate or whose parents were estate workers could be offered positions as boot- or hall-boys, with the potential to work their way up to become footman or even butler.

The passing of the 1870 Education Act led to the school-leaving age being raised several times in the late Victorian period and to an increase in school places for children. In 1880, full-time education was made compulsory for children up to the age of ten, and this was subsequently raised to 11 in 1893, then 12 in 1899. The school-leaving age was increased again to 14 under further legislation in 1918 (although it was not implemented until 1921). This clearly had a big impact on the age at which a child could start work and on the number of young girls available for domestic service.

However, before 1880, there was no official school-leaving age and parents could withdraw their children from education whenever they chose to. This was especially true for working-class families who frequently relied on the extra income children could earn. Elementary education was not made free of charge until 1891, so until that point a family's ability to fund attendance directly influenced the length of time a child remained in school. As a benchmark, workhouse children, who were given a rudimentary education by the Poor Law authorities, were apprenticed or sent into service from the age of 11 to 13, around the same age most working-class children still living in the family home started work.

For many parents, educating their daughters was less important than educating their sons, who would potentially be higher earners and therefore able to contribute more to the family's coffers. The age at which a girl was sent to her first place as a servant often depended very much on her family's financial circumstances. In 1800, Mary Ann Ashford was forced to find her own way in the world when she was orphaned at the age of 13. She had previously attended a charity school, but life changed irrevocably when her father's business failed and he developed a serious health condition, leading to his early demise. Hannah Cullwick was just eight years old when she entered domestic service in 1841. Although her father was a master saddler, trade constantly fluctuated, and with five children to provide for money was always tight, so Hannah's wages were a necessary contribution to the family income.

By contrast, in cases where a girl was useful to her parents in helping to run the home or assist in a family trade, there was no insistence for her to go into service and the idea was positively discouraged. In other families, domestic service was seen as irrevocably working-class, drastically reducing the chance to 'better' oneself. For young women who yearned for independence, however, domestic service represented an escape from parental control. Amy Grace Rose and Louise Jermy were both comparatively old when they went to their first place. Louise was 16 when she finally left the unhappy home where she had suffered physical abuse at the hands of her stepmother. The decision to leave was even harder for her because she had been partially disabled by tubercular hip disease three years earlier. At 22, Amy was a very late starter in domestic service, having previously stayed at home to do the cooking and cleaning, and to help her mother look after two babies she had taken in to nurse.

Finding a Place

A girl's first place in service was usually found by her parents, a teacher, or a charity. Parents frequently gained employment for their daughters through family connections or word of mouth. When an older sibling or cousin worked in a particular household, they were in a good position to recommend a younger relative for a job. Similarly, in small communities where everyone was well-known to one another, the vicar's wife, for example, could find a place in service for the daughter of a parishioner.

Mistresses or upper servants might mention to their local tradesmen that they were looking for a maid, and this information would be passed on. In her *Book of Household Management* (1861), Isabella Beeton recommended that:

> *the mistress to make inquiry amongst her circle of friends and acquaintances, and her tradespeople. The latter generally know those in their neighbourhood, who are wanting situations, and will communicate with them, when a personal interview with some of them will enable the mistress to form some idea of the characters of the applicants.*

Another way to find a place in service was through a servants' registry office. Dating back to the late eighteenth century, these offices operated in the same way as modern employment agencies. From the mid-Victorian period, there was a proliferation of new registries in large cities and smaller provincial market towns. They were frequently run by people who had retired from domestic service and therefore knew the qualities required of servants; smaller offices were often set up in tandem with another business, such as a newsagent or stationer.

Ladies who wanted new staff would contact a servants' registry with their requirements, details of the role on offer and the salary provided. In wealthy households with a large staff, the housekeeper or butler would be in charge of sourcing new servants, not the mistress. The office would match up servants with employers, and the larger ones supplied private booths in which prospective maids could be interviewed. In most cases, both mistress and servant would pay a fee for the service. Charities also ran registries, such as the Girls' Friendly Society, the Metropolitan Association for Befriending Young Servants (MABYS) and the Young Women's Christian Association (YWCA).

Some servants' registry offices catered purely for a higher class clientele and therefore only accepted servants with the very best employment records. Mrs Hunt's in Marylebone, one of the largest in London from the mid-nineteenth century and into the twentieth, fell under this category and offered a 'no engagement, no fee' policy to servants. While there were blacklists for unreliable and untrustworthy servants, perhaps surprisingly, similar lists were circulated among servants of households who treated their servants badly.

Some servants' registry offices had dubious reputations and there were frequent complaints about non-existent job vacancies. The *Pall Mall Gazette* (15 January 1894) explained how such scams worked:

> *Tempting advertisements are inserted in provincial newspapers. When servants answer them they are summoned to London by the registry-keeper who has advertised. On arrival in London, the deluded servants are unable to get any information about the situation advertised. The situations, in fact, do not exist, the servants having been deluded into coming up in order that they should lodge at the registry office, at a charge leaving a fine margin of profit to the keeper. Nor do they get a room to themselves at these so-called servants' homes. Seven, eight and nine are packed into one room, and the poor victims can do nothing but remonstrate, fearing that if they leave their chances of obtaining the desired situation will be made so much the more remote ... Servants lodging at these wretched homes are sent to employers where they cannot stop. For instance, a good servant is sent to a bad place, where he or she will not remain, and a bad servant is sent to a good place, where the master or mistress will not put up with incompetency. Thus the poor servants are constantly kept returning to the registry lodgings, impoverishing themselves while enabling these land-sharks to live in luxury.*

Fraudulent registry offices remained a problem throughout the period because the sector was unregulated. From 1907, those within the London County Council area were licensed annually and these licenses were withdrawn if there were complaints. However, local authorities elsewhere in Britain did not take advantage of powers to do the same, so the proprietor of a registry office in London with a revoked license could legally set up again outside the capital.

An even more popular way of finding a place was to peruse the 'Situations Vacant' columns in national and provincial newspapers; servants' registries also advertised here, often in discreetly worded messages placed on behalf of the gentry. For mistresses, it was a tried and tested method of finding good servants; *The Morning Post* and *The Times* were particularly well regarded sources for this.

Advertisements placed by prospective employers could be extremely specific about the attributes required in a servant, right down to age, height and physical appearance. This was particularly the case for visible 'above stairs' servants, such as footmen and parlourmaids, as seen in this example from *The Times* (31 August 1880):

PARLOURMAID for a gentleman's family in the country (Lincolnshire) REQUIRED at once. A little housework, with attendance on a lady. An excellent waitress. Good character and nice appearance indispensable. Height 5ft 5. Age from 25. Wages £20, all found. Address, E.M., Becklands, near Grimsby.

'All found' usually meant that tea, sugar, beer and washing would be provided by the employer in addition to the servant's wages, plus all meals and lodging. Some advertisements specified 'no beer', while others listed wages without any extra allowances.

Many wealthy households kept a pair of footmen and, when advertising for a new one, they specified an exact height so that their male servants would match. Footmen were given livery to wear when undertaking their duties, which could be handed on to their successor if they were of a similar size.

Employers might also recommend an ex-servant in an advertisement if, for example, they were moving abroad or there had been a change in family circumstances, as in this advertisement from *The Times* (4 May 1847):

A LADY is desirous of procuring a SITUATION for a highly respectable middle-aged PERSON, who is leaving her present situation on account of a death in the family. She has waited on the lady and acted as housekeeper during five years, and could be strongly recommended for the same service, or as housekeeper to a single gentleman, she being thoroughly conversant with household matters. Direct to J.M., Moore's library, 71, Lisson-grove, Marylebone.

In the late 1880s, some employers added 'no fringes' in their criteria, in reference to a particular women's hairstyle popular at the time. This was perhaps because they feared that servants with fringes would be more concerned about their appearance than their work. Many advertisements stated 'country girls preferred', because maids from rural areas were considered less flighty, more biddable and less ambitious than their city cousins.

Servants were always on the lookout for that elusive comfortable place with a considerate employer, where the pay was generous and working conditions were fair, and they had no qualms about changing jobs frequently. If they could not find one through the usual channels, then they could advertise for a place in the 'Situations Wanted' column of a local or national newspaper, although there was a charge to do so. *The Times* encouraged servants to advertise in its columns, arguing that it was in their interest to find a place with an employer who read an expensive, high quality newspaper.

Farm servants secured their employment for the coming year at the annual statute or hiring fairs in market towns (also sometimes called mop fairs), which were usually held in September or October. This tradition was kept up until the end of the nineteenth century.

A Good 'Character'

In order to be able to move on to a place with higher pay or better prospects, servants needed a good 'character'. This was the reference that employers provided when a servant left their household, and it was always highlighted as a positive trait whenever servants placed their own advertisements in the 'Situations Wanted' columns.

In her *Book of Household Management*, Mrs Beeton advised mistresses supplying references to former servants to:

> be guided by a sense of strict justice. It is not fair for one lady to recommend to another, a servant she would not keep herself. It is hardly necessary to remark, on the other hand, that no angry feelings on the part of a mistress towards her late servant, should ever be allowed, in the slightest degree, to influence her, so far as to induce her to disparage her maid's character.

There was no legal requirement for mistresses to provide references, giving them additional power over servants. If a character was not forthcoming, then any future employer would automatically assume that the servant was an unsatisfactory employee. By the same token, a mistress might write an untruthfully positive reference just to be rid of a troublesome maid, passing the problem on to the next employer. Written characters were also easy for servants to forge.

The expansion of the railway network from the mid-nineteenth century onwards made it far easier for servants to move out of their localities in search of better opportunities. London and other large cities were magnets, as were tourist resorts such as Blackpool or Brighton. As early as 1851, servants represented 39,000 of the 115,000 women in London aged between 15 and 20, of all classes. However, applying for a job advertised in a newspaper from a distance had its pitfalls because the details could be extremely misleading, especially for those lacking local knowledge or contacts. It was easy for an employer to misrepresent a vacancy, describing a place as one thing when it was in fact entirely different, yet, the servant had little choice but to carry on with the new job or risk losing their character.

When reading servants' memoirs or oral histories, the precariousness of their employment is particularly striking. There was no job security whatsoever; servants were always at the mercy of their employers' lifestyle or state of mind. A servant could be dismissed if their mistress was moving house and did not want to take her old staff; if a change in the household's financial circumstances required a reduction in the number of servants; or simply if their employer was not happy with the service they provided. Legally, servants could be dismissed instantly for insubordination or 'defiance to proper orders'. In so many ways, servants lived their lives never knowing from one day to the next what the future would hold.

Lower servants' jobs depended on maintaining good working relationships with upper servants and employers. A simple misunderstanding, a quick temper or a cross word were all easily magnified in a household where staff had nowhere to let off steam and limited opportunities to get away from the workplace. Even if a maid was in a good place and giving satisfactory service, she could still be given notice, for instance, if someone who had worked in the household previously had suddenly become available again.

The main perk of live-in employment – the fact that board and lodging were provided – was a double-edged sword, as it meant that the majority of servants had no home of their own. On finding themselves unexpectedly between jobs, their paltry savings could quickly be spent in paying for lodgings and they could easily become homeless if they had no relatives or friends to stay with while looking for another situation. Many desperate out-of-place servants were tempted into prostitution just to survive.

For some, domestic service represented the opportunity to escape an unhappy home life. Yet, for those with an aptitude for learning who wanted to continue their education but could not do so because of the cost, going into service was a personal sacrifice. Duty to one's parents and contributing to the family finances had to come first. Jessie Stephen was destined to be a schoolteacher and had a scholarship to secondary school but had to leave at the age of 15:

> trade was so bad that particular year [1908], I had to go out to work. I went to one or two jobs, factory jobs, but it was only half a crown a week and I wasn't helping Mother. So I said I'll find a job in service because at any rate the money will be completely free of any expense to Mother. Of course, you'd have your

board and lodging ... I am grateful to my Dad. He cried a bit when I said I was
going ... he wanted something better for me but of course in later years, I justified
his appreciation of what I'd learned. (Recorded interview from LSE Library's
collections, ref: 8SUF/B/157, 1 July 1977.)

Marriage provided a way out from the drudgery of service for many women, who
found they resented being at the beck and call of an employer at all hours. The
unremitting toil expected from maids was the cause of many a hasty wedding
and subsequently unhappy marriage.

The First Place

When going into service for the first time, the new servant underwent a kind
of apprenticeship and, as he or she had everything to learn, they were not well
paid. A report in 1899 found that the average wage of female general servants
under the age of 16 in England and Wales (excluding London) was just £6 5s
per annum (or 2s 4d per week). In the capital, the Metropolitan Association for
Befriending Young Servants recommended a wage of £6 3s for a girl in her first
position, while in Glasgow, Edinburgh and Dundee the average starting wage
was slightly higher at £7 3s.

These young girls had usually never been away from the parental home before.
Now, off they went with their boxes (in which all their worldly belongings were
kept) to live in a strange household, working for people they did not know. A
great deal was expected of them and it was extremely tough for a girl going to
her first place, especially if she was to be a single-handed 'general' or 'maid of all
work', with no other servants to show her the ropes. She may have been taught
how to cook and clean at home by her mother, but it was a completely different
situation when asked to do the same in a larger house with more delicate china
and furnishings.

For some, the first experience of domestic service was positively traumatic.
Mrs Wrigley, a plate layer's wife, was born in Cefn Mawr, Wales in 1858. In
Life As We Have Known It, edited by Margaret Llewelyn Davies, Mrs Wrigley
recalled how she was sent to her first proper place at the tender age of nine,
ostensibly to be a nursemaid:

Instead of being a nurse I had to be a servant-of-all-work, having to get up at
six in the morning, turn a room out and get it ready for breakfast. My biggest
trouble was I could not light the fire, and my master was very cross and would

tell me to stand away, and give me a good box on my ears ... I fretted very much for my home. Humble as it was, it was home. Not able to read or write, I could not let my parents know, until a kind old lady in the village wrote to my parents to fetch me home from the hardships I endured. I had no wages at this place, only a few clothes.

When a daughter followed in her mother's footsteps by going into service, hints and tips were undoubtedly passed on, although rarely recorded in writing. The following letter was sent around 1868 by Louisa Mist (née Angel) to her granddaughter Topsy Dorcas Mist, then aged 12 or 13, after Topsy had gone into service for the first time. Topsy worked for a Miss Prewett, who ran a grocer's shop and lived with her brother and widowed mother in Godshill, Hampshire. It is likely that Topsy was employed as a general servant in the house and to look after the elderly mother, while Miss Prewett ran the shop. Only a fragment of the original letter remains:

O my Child do keep your Place, Such A good Place and Miss Pruet in her letter said she assisted you to make your Frock and I make no doubt but that she would Show you to make your things too and such good wages for A Girl of your age I hope you will keep your Place A long time and if you are not let out on Sundays only to church what A good thing how many temptations you escape by being quiet at home how many Poor thoughtless Girls are led into trouble through being let out to range about Sunday nights and tis Breaking the Sabbath to which God forbids he says Remember the Sabbath Day to keep it holy which you could not do if you was out amixing A giddy Company of young people in conversation and no doubt some vain talk which would not be Proper on the Sabbath Day. Please give my kindest love and Respect to Miss Pruet and your fellow servant and accept the same from your Loving Grandmother L Mist.

Topsy did keep her place but when Mrs Prewett died two years later, she returned home to her grandparents' farm. Her grandfather died the same year and Louisa passed away in 1872. At some point Topsy went back into domestic service, as she was working at Breamore House in the New Forest when she met her future husband Alfred Palmer, who was a gardener there. The couple married in 1878.

The Employers

While entering gentlemen's service was the goal of every ambitious servant, the majority did not work for such illustrious employers. Most toiled in much smaller households employing just one or two servants. Their employers included the professional classes, such as doctors, lawyers and clergy; the upwardly-mobile middle classes, such as bank managers, clerks and schoolmasters; as well as tradesmen and shopkeepers. Hotels, schools and hospitals also employed servants, while positions at farms and lodging houses were usually at the bottom of the scale.

Dozens of manuals and guides were published for middle-class readers who had never kept servants before and now found themselves in a position to do so. These included Mrs Beeton's *Book of Household Management* (1861), Mrs Florence Caddy's *Household Organisation* (1877), and Mrs J. E. Panton's *From Kitchen to Garret* (1888). They provided advice on every aspect of servants' duties, household rules, and even the correct etiquette for hiring and dismissing staff.

It was during the 1850s and 1860s that the phenomenon of the middle classes employing servants really developed. Domestic help was cheap and plentiful until the end of the nineteenth century, and families with any kind of social pretensions kept at least one servant, preferably two. As a very visible status symbol, they helped to cement one's place in Victorian society, but taking on a servant was not just a case of keeping up appearances. Before central heating, hot running water and washing machines, servants provided essential assistance in running a home, especially if there were a large number of children in the household.

Male Servants

Male servants invariably received higher salaries than their female equivalents and, as employers had to pay a tax on them, they were only employed by the wealthy. As such, they were even more of a status symbol than maids. When Clara Collet undertook her survey for the Board of Trade, *Money Wages of Indoor Domestic Servants* in 1899, she discovered that, on average, butlers earned £58 6s per annum, footmen £26 7s and men-servants with undefined duties, £38 6s. The majority of male domestic servants, she noted, worked in 'large households employing over six servants, and the vails received by them [were] a very much larger item in their earning than in the case of women in such households.'

'Vails' were the tips that footmen, valets and butlers expected to receive from house-guests as payment for the extra duties undertaken for them.

Throughout the nineteenth and twentieth centuries, there was a gradual trend for male servants to be replaced by women because they were cheaper to employ and were considered easier to manage. Instead of a footman, middle-class households might employ a parlourmaid to greet visitors and undertake valeting duties, as well as a boy to polish the knives and boots. In 1891, just 54 per 10,000 of the male population over the age of 10 were employed in indoor domestic service; by contrast, 1,169 per 10,000 females were similarly employed. Male servants did, however, continue to be in demand as outdoor servants on landed estates, as gardeners, grooms and, later, chauffeurs.

Career Servants

For the ambitious servant, there was a defined path for career progression for both men and women, particularly within larger aristocratic households. A footman could work his way up to under-butler, then butler, while a scullery maid could be promoted to kitchen-maid and then plain cook in a smaller household. If a housemaid or parlourmaid was literate and a good needlewoman, then she could hope to be promoted to housekeeper or lady's maid.

According to Mrs Beeton, in 1861 a kitchen-maid might be paid between £8 and £12 when an extra allowance was made for tea, sugar and beer, while a cook could receive from £12 to £26, depending on experience. An upper housemaid's wages were between £10 and £17, while a housekeeper's salary was in the range of £18 to £40. In addition to higher wages, upper servants also obtained the privilege of having their own room.

Gaining a promotion usually meant moving to another establishment, as there were rarely opportunities for advancement within the same household; this was particularly the case for male servants because fewer vacancies existed in the first place. Career progression was more limited for those working in domestic service for the middle classes. Indeed, it was almost impossible for single-handed generals or those working in two servant households to move on to working in larger establishments paying more generous wages. Clara Collet attributed their disqualification from such promotion to 'the want of "professional" training', which she considered 'a serious defect in our social organisation'.

Servants' Duties

The duties servants performed and their working hours depended very much on their particular role within the household, and how many other members of domestic staff were kept. It was well-known that a nursemaid's position was a good first place for a young girl, provided she did not have to do the cooking and cleaning as well. A housemaid, on the other hand, had a very long working day, especially during the winter months, when much of her time was taken up with laying fires in numerous rooms and keeping them alight throughout the day.

In a large country house, there was a very strict hierarchy between servants who all had specific roles in separate 'departments' of the house. They had to make sure that the routines of the house ran like clockwork, and tasks were frequently divided between a number of different staff working in the same role. For instance, a head housemaid might have a second, third or even fourth housemaid working under her direction, or a cook could be assisted by a kitchen-maid and scullery maid. The same was true of male servants, with a butler in charge of an under butler, first footman and second footman.

In the smaller middle-class household, there was less of a distinction between roles and servants had to undertake numerous tasks they would never be expected to do in a larger house. A single-handed male servant in a more modest household might have the nominal title of butler, but he would have been carrying out tasks associated with a butler, footman and valet combined, as well as plenty of arduous work usually assigned to a boot or knife boy.

The Social Status of Servants

In certain sections of upper working-class and lower middle-class society, there was an unspoken stigma associated with being a servant. After she was orphaned in 1800, tradesman's daughter Mary Ann Ashford was warned against going into service by other members of her family, who wanted her to undertake an apprenticeship in needlework instead:

A cousin of my mother's ... pointed out to me, in strong terms, the folly of opposing the good intentions of my friends: she said a great deal about injuring my future prospects, as I could not be introduced into society by her or any of my respectable friends if I was a servant. Now, I was too young and too simple to understand much about it, for it was almost like Greek and Latin to me: however, I gleaned from her majestic oration, that, in the event of my being out of place, they would have nothing to do with me.

This view that servants should be looked down upon because of their servitude was not one shared by footman William Tayler, although he did make a distinction between ordinary and gentlemen's servants. In his diary entry for 14 May 1837, Tayler commented,

> *everyone must think and must know that [gentlemen's] servants form one of the most respectable classes of persons that is in existance [sic]. In the first place, they must be healthy, clean, respectable, honest, sober set of people to be servants; their character must be unexceptionable in every respect … Being so much in the company of the gentry, from the private gentleman to the highest Duke in the land allways [sic] traveling about with their masters, learning and seeing hundreds of things which mecanics [sic] and tradespeople never knew there was.*

The 'stigma' of being a servant remained a problem throughout the period 1800–1950 for employers wanting to attract new recruits to the occupation, and no amount of pay or good working conditions could erase it.

Mary Ann Ashford

General Servant, Housemaid and Cook

Born in London in 1787, Mary Ann Ashford was the daughter of a tradesman. She and her younger brother were orphaned in 1800 when their mother died and their father passed away a few months later. At the age of 13, Mary went into domestic service, an occupation she followed until her marriage in 1817.

This extract is taken from her autobiography, *The Life of a Licensed Victualler's Daughter, Written by Herself* (1844) and is reproduced by kind permission of the British Library. © The British Library Board (Shelfmark 1202.h.30)

In a few days after [my father died], it was considered by my relations ... what was to be done with me; it appeared that they proposed to contribute amongst them as much money as would place me as an in-door apprentice to a dressmaker or milliner, for at least five years. When I was informed of their kind intentions, I went to Mrs Bond, who was an old friend and countrywoman of my father's, to tell her.

She said, "I'll tell thee what, Polly, that is all very well for those who have got a house and parents to shelter them, when work is slack; but depend upon it, many clever women find it, at times, a half-starved kind of life in those employments. Now, thee art a hearty, well-grown girl, and I think would be better off in service, but you had better go and consult your father's aunt Margaret, and hear what she says about it."

This I very soon did, and told her they wished to place me out genteelly. She said that was all very fine, but there was an old and very true proverb, that "gentility without ability, was like a pudding without fat" and she was of Mrs Bond's opinion.

I could at that time work at my needle very well, but at the same time, I did not much like it; so, my own inclination agreeing with their advice, I resolved to take it ... to the utter astonishment of all parties [I] declared my intention of going into service ... Just at this time, a man called at Mr Batt's [*the church clerk in whose home she was then staying*] ... to enquire for a servant; ... I went with him to a house in Exchange Alley, that had just opened as a banking-house; he took me to the head clerk, who said his wife and family were coming in a few days, and he supposed I could do the work; but he never asked my age, which was not more than thirteen years and three months; however, he hired me at six pounds ten shillings a year; and I suppose he thought he had got a much better bargain than I turned out to be ...

The next evening I went, and in a few days my mistress and four lovely children arrived; and, as I was very tall for my age, she had no idea I was little more than a child myself, but she soon found it out ... I did the best I could, notwithstanding I had cut my hand, very badly, in splitting firewood. When I had been there about two months, it was reported in the neighbourhood that the banking-house had merely been opened to swindle a young man of fortune out of his money. When Mr Batt heard of it, he desired me to tell my mistress that I must leave her; which I did, as soon as she got a servant ...

I was again pressed to give up my intentions of going to service, but I remained in the same mind, and my relations gave up the contest and saved their money. I got a place soon after, at Hoxton, with the wife of the then head waiter of Garraway's Coffee House ... I remained in this place till I was near sixteen, my wages commencing at two pounds ten shillings, rising a pound a year. My mistress here made me nurse the child, and do everything that was laborious; but all that required any art or knowledge, she not only would not let me do, but would send me out of the way, with the little boy, while she did it herself. This was done that I should not leave her, or think myself qualified for a better place. In the winter, water used to come into the cellars; and I have been bolted in them for hours together, till I have been nearly exhausted with pumping, and almost poisoned with the smell: however, I was well fed. One August, I gave warning, as I would not run the risk of another winter's pumping.

I left Hoxton in September, 1803, and ... heard of a nursemaid's place at Bromley: I saw the lady, and agreed to go for a month upon trial; and being shy and diffident, I, simpleton-like, never said a word about wages; and when the month was up, she said I suited her very well indeed, and she should give me five pounds a year, out of which I was to find my own tea and sugar. I made no objection then but I soon considered that it would never find me in apparel; and it was too far for those friends who used sometimes to make me presents, to assist me while I had low wages. I therefore gave my mistress warning. She seemed sadly vexed; and I left her at the end of ten weeks.

During that time they had no less than five foot-boys; it was one of those places that have got a bad name; and that is worse in the country than in London; and servants are often very silly in that respect, and, instead of looking to the treatment they receive themselves, listen to what other people say. But it was not the case with me, as I left on account of the low wages ...

In a day or two, I went to London to my old friend, and ... was very diligent in seeking a place. And I got one to go to on the third of December, with an old lady who lived in the City Terrace, in the City Road. I set to work the next day to clean the house, which was very dirty with her being so long alone ...

This lady, who was very much in years ... had been long a widow and was very kind to me in manner, but she was penurious in the extreme. The family consisted of my mistress and myself, and a gentleman who was the minister of the Scotch Church in London Wall; he occupied three rooms, with attendance; there was besides, a monkey, two dogs, a cat, and many birds, all of which I had to attend to. My mistress had very high connections, and used to spend her time very much among them, and she would be away for days and weeks together, and leave me with very little to subsist on, and with orders to give "Jacko" the best of everything.

The gentleman who lived in the house, when he had no invitations, used to dine at home, sometimes two or three times a week, and he seldom ate the whole of his chops or steaks, and what he left used to eke out my very frugal dinners. I think he suspected that I was kept very short, and was always very civil to me.

After this my mistress said she had lost a good counterpane, and the servant I had succeeded must have taken it away with her. I offered to go and let her know, that she might give an account of it; for I thought it a sad thing to be falsely accused. She came, and ... this brought about a reconciliation between my mistress and her; for she had lived with her a long time, and they had parted in a sudden quarrel; and after that ... I could hardly ever do anything to please her. The old servant was certainly more suitable for the place than I was. As she was above forty years old, I dare say her appetite was not so sharp as that of a girl not seventeen.

If she had said she was going to have Sarah back, it would have been all very well, and she need not have fallen out with me; but I am sorry to say that many ladies, when they wish to part with a servant who is not guilty of a particular fault, instead of being candid, and warning them to quit, they find fault about trifles, and tease and aggravate them to give warning themselves.

[*Mary's mistress blamed her when one of the little dogs disappeared and when a goldfinch escaped from its cage, and accused her of ill-using the monkey when she was absent. Mary was also tempted to eat some of the lodger's cheese out of hunger.*]

I shall never forget how enraged and aghast he looked when he saw its shrunken dimensions. When his dinner was over, he went to my mistress and laid a heavy complaint against me, and, what was worse, insinuated that she ought to make good the damage; for if the girl had been properly fed, he did not think she would have taken his cheese, as he had left much nicer things in her way, such as wine, sugar and biscuits.

This was enough to raise a storm, and in the midst of it I gave warning, and left when the month was up; and a weary month of it I had. My mistress deducted from my wages for every little thing I had broken during the seven months I had been with her, and her old servant came every day and made what mischief she could ...

The gentleman, who seemed very sorry for me, in spite of the cheese affair, told me to go to a house in Artillery Place, where the lady wanted a housemaid. It was at a West India merchant's and I was to succeed a young woman who had left, intending to marry ... Here I might have done very well, but in a little time my mistress told me that the young woman who left to be married had fallen out with her intended, and wished to come back; and as she had been with her two years ... she meant to take her back again ...

I went to mind some children for a short time, and then to stop with a lady whose servant was ill; and with one thing or other, was very unsettled for some months. [But] I resolved to seek a regular service.

One of my old friends in the city sent me after a housemaid's place at No. 10 Lambeth Terrace. The lady, who was a clergyman's widow, said she gave £7 a year to a housemaid, but if I would take the place as servant-of-all-work for a time, she would give at the rate of nine guineas a year, as part of her family was absent. Now this to me was a very great offer [and] I told her that I was quite willing to agree to her terms, but was afraid I could not manage the cooking. She said she would instruct me.

I went there on the 7th of February, 1805. Here I worked very hard, but my mistress, who was an excellent manager, regulated my work, so that I took no harm; but I heard that she used to have many servants in a year. How it was I do not know, for she was very kind indeed to me, and bitterly I repented leaving her, which I did in six months, having been persuaded by a nursemaid at the next door ...

I gave Mrs Pearce warning, and very much vexed she was ... I soon found I had made a bad exchange, except in wages, which was ten guineas a year, and to be raised if I stopped. My mistress soon began to tyrannize over me by scolding almost continually ... I asked the nursemaid how she could have been so unkind as to persuade me to leave a place that was to me so much more pleasant, to come into such a turmoil. She said she would not deny it, but she did it for her own sake ... We had very bad living; very little meat, and the bread kept till it was mould before it was cut ...

I made a great many attempts to leave her, by giving warning, and going after other places; but when the ladies came for my character, she always said something that broke it off ... I was sadly vexed ... and Heaven knows how much longer I should have been there, had not a lady in Canterbury Place, just opposite, married, which made a change in the domestic arrangements of the family. I went to speak with Mrs W___, and she was much pleased, and said she would wait a month for me, as she had heard Mrs Pearce ... speak very highly of me ...

In this place I remained nearly three years and a half: my mistress was kind to me beyond everything, and I had a most excellent place. The starving places I had been in had the good effect of making me really economical in everything that came under my care, and that I had the use of ... But there was one thing I could never reconcile myself to: a great part of the time I was in the house by myself; for my mistress used to go out a great deal, often being at her sister's for days and weeks together. I was not afraid of being in the house alone but it made me feel so dull ...

I mentioned it to my mistress, who, after that, used to let me sit and work with her, when she was at home; and the third summer I was there, she went to Brighton, and took me with her. At the lodgings ... there was but one kitchen, and that occupied by the persons of the house, I therefore resided with them; and there were four in the family, besides many acquaintances who used to come in. We were there three weeks; and when I came home, the change I had seen made my situation seem more irksome than ever ...

I stopped nearly a year after, and then I mustered courage enough to tell my good and kind mistress that I must leave her, for the frequent solitude I could no longer bear; and I left a good home.

I had the offer, through Mrs Pearce, of the cook's place, at Alderman Goodbehere's on China Terrace, but I was afraid to take it, thinking I could never cook for an alderman, as my knowledge of cooking was very limited at that time; and I went as housemaid, in a Jew's family, in Leman Street, Goodman's Fields; but in a short time, I heard that there was great difficulty in getting a place, after living with Jews; and as Miss W___ had given me an excellent character, I could not think of losing it ...

My next place was with the head clerk of an eminent solicitor, in Great Winchester Street; and his wife and I agreed very well: but when I had been there about ten months, a cheese-monger's wife, in the same street, said to me one day, that she thought I might better myself, and if I liked, she would look out for a plain cook's place for me, among her customers.

As I was now near four-and-twenty, and ... had picked up a little knowledge of culinary matters, I felt much obliged to her; and in a short time she recommended me to a lady, whose daughter wanted a cook ... and I went to live at Staines, where there was a nurse and housemaid besides myself, and a lad who looked after the horse and chaise, worked in the garden and cleaned knives; and I got on tolerably well, considering it was my first cook's place; only I was obliged to submit very much to my fellow-servants, they having both lived with my mistress for a long time, and during her widowhood, as the gentleman was her second husband. They were both much older than I was; but as, at that time, I was pliable enough, I conformed to them pretty well, and thought to stop a twelvemonth.

When I had been there about eight months ... we had a few days' holiday each; and when [the other servants] returned, they brought word that a cook, who had married from my mistress, wished to leave her husband and come back to her again; but the master said I was a good servant, and she had better not part with me; but being resolved about it, she contrived to aggravate me till I gave her warning. I inquired about Staines, but did not hear of any place; and I had the sorry prospect of having to pay my own expenses to London, and employment to seek afterwards.

My time was nearly up, when it seemed that Providence interfered in my favour; for a lady and gentleman from Epsom came there on a visit, which they had never done before; and when I retired for the night, the housemaid said that she had a proposal to make to me from my mistress, which was, that the visitors were going to part with their cook and housemaid, and keep one thorough servant; and the stable lad to come and assist in the house; they would give me the same wages I had, and if I suited raise me two guineas a year; my present master would send me and my luggage to Kingston, and they would send the chaise there to take me to Epsom.

I went to Epsom the 4th of May 1812, and never had so agreeable a change: they were very pleasant people to live with, and I gave them great satisfaction and did their work with pleasure ... Soon after this my master and mistress removed into the Hackney Road ... When we left Epsom, the servant lad was parted with, and a girl kept instead ... In a few months later, my mistress intended to part with the girl and keep only one servant, and I declined stopping by myself.

By this time, my father's aunt Margaret had become very old and infirm, and it was a long way from Hackney to Brompton, where she had lived for many years; and I thought if I could get nearer to her, it would be a comfort to us both ... My mistress wishing to send me with a message to a friend of hers at Chelsea, I was to have the rest of the day to myself, to look after a place. I did not begin to inquire till I got into the City Road ... I went into many shops and heard of many cooks' places, and, I think, went after nine or ten, but did not engage with any; there was either something that I did not suit them, or they did not suit me. At a shop in Knightsbridge, I was directed to a doctor's in Great Sloane Street, in want of a cook; and just as I was about to ring the bell, a cheese-monger came up the area steps; he whispered to me, "Are you coming after the place?"

I said, "Yes."

"Then you can do as you like," said he, "but you may as well live with old Nick as come here; for they have had four cooks in three months."

With this hint I walked on; and [when] it was near dark ... I came to a greengrocer's shop ... The shopkeeper said he did not know of a cook's place; [then remembered] who it was that had asked for one. It was at a clergyman's, in a large national institution, which I shall call Fairy Land [*believed to be the Royal Military Asylum*]; it being inhabited, at that time, by above twelve hundred soldiers' children, their officers and attendants. I went and saw the lady: she asked me many questions, all of which I answered to her apparent satisfaction ... she expressed herself satisfied in a letter she wrote to my mistress, whom I had lived with a year and nine months, for my character, and it was answered highly in my favour ... we agreed that I was to go to her on the same day that I quitted the Hackney Road, which I did on the 12th of February, 1814 ...

When the year was up I had not the least inclination to leave; but when I had been there about a year and a half, my employers were about to keep two female servants instead of three, and as the housemaid to whom I was most attached was to leave, and there was to be many fresh regulations, I said I would leave likewise, and I went to live at Edgeware.

But I had not been there many weeks, when I received a letter from the nurse to say that my late mistress had got a cook who did not suit her at all, and if I was not suited in my place, and had any inclination to come back again, she was certain I might ... I went back to Fairy Land and made myself quite contented, and became thoroughly attached to the whole family ...

In August 1817, my master went abroad, and my mistress, with a Mrs M, went to Brighton for a month, taking me with them. This lady had six children, a young lady companion, and two nurses, with the servant lad, my own mistress and two of her boys, making altogether fifteen in family. The whole of the domestic work was done by me and the lad, as the nurses were fully occupied with the children; and very heavy work it was ... I have often wondered how I managed to do it, and I was very glad to get home again. When we had returned a few days, my mistress went to visit her brother at Sunning Hill; she took the children with her, and parted from me in the kindest manner imaginable, telling me that, if I liked, I might go out for a day or two.

[*A few days later, Mary received a letter from her mistress giving her a month's notice as she had heard that a servant she had long wanted to engage was available.*]

I think I never felt more grieved and surprised in my life ... I was now near thirty years old, seventeen years of that time I had spent in service and never had warning given to me before; and if I had served one mistress better than another, it was my present one ... Had I been accused of any fault, I might have apologised or cleared myself, as the case might be; but I had now no alternative but to do as I was bid, and get another place ...

When I had about a fortnight to stop, I gave [my fellow house-servant] a pair of boots, and asked him to take them to the shoemaker [James Dallison], and tell him to put a good strong pair of heels on them, for I was going to seek my fortune ... A day or two after he said the master shoemaker wanted to speak to me ... I went in ... [and he said] that if I had a mind to marry, and would have him, he would have me. I was much surprised ... He then [said] if I should consent it would be no use for me to think of getting another place, and we had better be married as soon as possible ...

I resolved to accept the old soldier's offer ... A few days after I left, and returned to Chelsea, and was married on the 3rd of November, 1817, at Chelsea old church.

Mary and James had six children, one of whom died aged two, and she was widowed in 1829, remarrying the following year. It is believed that she died in the 1840s.

William Tayler

Footman and Butler

Born in 1807 in rural Oxfordshire, William Tayler worked as a footman in London for the wealthy widow Mrs Prinsep and her unmarried daughter. He kept a diary for the year 1837, 'as I am a wretched bad writer [and] many of my friends have advised me to practice more.' On Sundays, he usually went to see his wife and children who were lodged nearby, although he never referred to her or them by name; he was clearly earning a sufficient salary to pay their rent. The diary gives an illuminating insight into the life of a male servant for the gentry during the early nineteenth century, including details of what William did in his spare time and how the wealthy entertained.

The following extract has been taken from *Diary of William Tayler, Footman 1837* edited by Dorothy Wise, with notes by Ann Cox-Johnson (published by the St Marylebone Society, 1987). It has been reproduced with the kind permission of the St Marylebone Society. Original spellings have been retained throughout.

January 1st, 1837 ... I am the only man-servant kept here as the coachman is only a sort of jobber. Here are three maidservants, very quiet good sort of bodys, and we live very comfortable together. Here is only a mistress and her daughter, the first a widdow and the latter an old maid. She is at least forty years of age, therefore I think she deserves that title. They are also very quiet good sort of people but very gay and sees a great deal of company ... The father is dead and so are two of the sons; their widows are very often visiting here as well as some of the other sons' children – much oftner than we want them. The latter are here at present during the holidays.

The first of January is ushered in with very cold frost and snow. This being Sunday, nothing has transpired of consequence. I got up at half past seven, cleaned the boys' clothes and knives [and] lamps, got the parlour breakfast, lit my pantry fire, cleared breakfast and washed it away, dressed myself, went to church, came back, got parlour lunch, had my own dinner, sat by the fire and red the Penny Magazine and opened the door when any visitors came. At 4 o'clock had my tea, took the lamps and candles up into the drawing room, shut the shutters, took glass, knives, plate and settera into the dining room, layed the cloth for dinner, took the dinner up at six o'clock, waited at dinner, brought the things down again at seven, washed them up, brought down the desert, got ready the tea, took it up at eight o'clock, brought it down at half past, washed up, had my supper at nine, took down the lamps and candles at half past ten and went to bed at eleven. All these things I have to do every day, therefore I have mentioned the whole that I mite not have to mention them every day.

4th. Got up at seven o'clock. This is a very buisy day, nothing but work all day – company to dinner in the parlour and a children's party in the evening, play acting and dancing and a grand supper. It's not fashionable for jentlefolk to have supper, only on such occasions as this. Did not get to bed until one o'clock and very tired.

10th. All the people in the house are ill with the influenza. The old Lady and two of the boys and one of the maids are ill in bed now, therefore we that are well have plenty to do to wait on the others. I cannot hardly leave the house in consequence, obliged to remain at home all this day, amused myself with drawing and reading. This evening the old lady thought herself worse; went for the doctor. He was gone to the play; came back – the patient is better and I am just going to bed.

15th. This being Sunday of course I went to church – or rather, I took a little walk elsewhere [*to see his wife and children*]. The old Lady, I am sory to say, gets worse; I am afraid we shall soon lose her. The cook is very ill too; she keeps her bed ...

16th. Got up at half past seven; done my usual work. The old Lady and cook both very ill in bed, the housemaid gone home to bury her Mother, the Lady's maid very ill but obliged to keep about – myself and Miss P. are the only two that has not had it. We expect to be caught hold of very soon. The Influenza was never known to be so bad as it is now ... I am obliged to stay within to help the sick. This is what I don't like as I like to get a run everyday when I can.

20th. Up at eight. The sick people are getting better, all but the old Lady; she is very poorly and I don't know which way she intend to take yet ...

22nd. This being Sunday of course I went to church. I think I will give an account of our liveing during the next week. They breakfast at eight in the kitchen on bread and butter and toast – or anything of the kind if they like to be at the trouble of making it – and tea. All most all servants are obliged to find their own tea and sugar. For my own part I care but very little about breakfast at all, therefore I jenerally wait until the breakfast comes down from the parlour at ten o'clock when my apatite has come and I can then git a cup of coco, which I am very fond of, and a rowl or something of the kind. Anyone that like to have lunch, there it is for them but, as I have breakfast so late, I want no lunch. This day we had for dinner a piece of surloin of beef, roasted brocoli and potatos and preserved damson pie. We all have tea together at four o'clock with bread and butter and sometimes a cake. At nine o'clock we have supper; this evening it's cold beef and damson pie. We keep plenty of very good table ale in the house and every one can have as much as they like. This has been a miserable wet day and I have spent most of it in reading the news paper.

February 17th. Went out this morning; bought myself a paire of knee buckles and some shoe ties; employed myself with drawing this afternoon and read this evening. Miss P. is gone to the next house to tea and I am waiting up for her to come home. She is just come and it's twelve o'clock and I am of to bed.

19th. This is Sunday, a wet boisterous day. Been to church of course. Our old Lady is got quite well, thinks of little elce but playing cards and paying visets all the time.

March 4th. I have been in this place two years this day and have just taken my quarter's wages which is ten guineas. Have been out with the carriage round Hyde Park; the wind was enough to blow one away. Been out to supper this evening.

9th. Had company to dinner and more to tea. I got one shilling out of the whole lot. It's quite out of the fashion to give anything to servants at such times. Got to bed at half past twelve.

14th. Went out this morning and got measured for a morning jacket, and went to Mr Puzey's and ordered a new hat …

17th. Been a little way in the Country with the carrige today; found it very cold. The tailor has brought home my jacket for which he want a sovering and I will only give him 19 shillings. Young Mr W. Puzey has just brought my hat which I have paid a guinea for according to agreement. Been out to supper.

April 25th. Went out with the carriage to take the Ladies to the Opra House to a consort. Came back and had my dinner and went with the carriage to take them up, and took Miss P. to her sister's in Belgrave Square where she staid to dinner and spent the evening there with many others. Went at half past twelve this night to fetch her home. It poured with rain. When I got there, I was ask into the inner apartments as I live with some of the famley. There was a large party of gents and ladies at supper. I went and looked in the room where they were forty sitting at supper; everything was butiful and splendid. These people very often gives such parties and they spare no expence; the best pastrey-cooks and confectioners are imploid in London. After I had looked at them and heard them sing some good songs, I went downstairs – first into the pantry where the footman gave me a tumbler of sherry which I drank. I then went into the housekeeper's room, and she gave me a tumbler of mulled port wine and a lot of sweetmeats which I very soon devoured. After sitting and talking to the ladiesmaids awhile, I went into the pantry again where the butler would insist on my haveing a glass of champagne, and after a little, he gave me a glass of sherrey. I then began to get very talkative and after helping wipe some of their glasses he gave me another glass of muld port and by the way of a finish he gave me a glass of sherey. By this time I am sertain I had drunk a bottle of wine and to get off from drinking more, I went up to the entrance hall to be out of the way … We got home a little before three o'clock.

26th. Got up early this morning to go to the coach with a Lady who was going in the country. She gave me half-a-crown and little enough. My head aches and I feel very poorly after drinking so much wine.

May 5th. Went out this morning, staid a long time. When I came home, the maidservants grumbled very much becaus I left them to answer all the doors and bells. Been out with the carriage this afternoon. They kept me out longer than usual and longer than I wished, therefore I shall talk to them about it another day.

10th. It's surpriseing to see the number of servants that are walking about the streets out of place … Servants are so plentifull that gentlefolk will only have those that are tall, upright, respectable-looking young people and must bare the very best character, and mechanics are so very numerous that most tradespeople sends their sons and daughters out to servise rather than put them to a trade. By that reason, London and every other tound is over run with servants.

14th. As the old Lady and her daughter are quite allone at present, there is not so much cooking for the parlour as there is in general. For the parlour breakfast, they have hot rolls, dry toast, a loaf of fancy bread and a loaf of common and a slice of butter. They have the hot water come up in a hurn that has a place in the middle for a red hot iron which keep the water boiling as long as the iron keep hot. With this, they make their tea themselves. They have chocolate which is something like coffee but of a greasey and much richer nature. This is all they have for breakfast, and it's the same every morning. They have it as soon as they are up, which is nine o'clock. It take them about three-quarters of an houre to breakfast.

Lunch at one, the same time we dine in the kitchen. They generally have some cut from ours or have cold meat and some vegitables. Dinner at six which is considered very early. This day they had two soles fryed with saws, a leg of mutton, a dish of ox, pullets, potatos, brocolo, rice and a rhubarb tart, a tabiaca pudding, cheese and butter. Has tea at eight o'clock with bread and butter and dry toast; never any supper – it's not fashionable.

18th. This is a very buisy day as we are going to have a party this evening something larger than usual. We had four to dinner and about fifty or sixty in the evening. The plan of manageing these parties are thus:- there were two men besides myself, one opened the door and let the Company in, I shewed them into a parlour where there was three maidservants to make tea and give it to them and take off their cloaks and bonnets, and the other man shewed them up into the drawingroom and gave in their names as lowd as he can bawl in the drawingroom. There is very good singing and music in their way. After they have been here some time, we carrey them up some refreshments on trays and hand about amongst them. This is all kinds of sweet cakes and biscuits, lemonade, ashet, negos, orangade and many other pleasent drinks but the best is the different kind of ices … The company comes jeneraly about ten or eleven o'clock and stays until one or two in the morning. Sweet hearting matches are very often made up at these parties. It's quite disgusting to a modist eye to see the way the young ladies dress to atract the notice of the gentlemen. They are nearly naked to the waist, only just a little bit of dress hanging on the shoulder, the breasts are quite exposed except a little bit comeing up to hide the nipples. Plenty of false haire and teeth and paint. If a person wish to see the ways of the world, they must be a gentleman's servant, then they mite see it to perfection … If we have a man to come to wait at dinner and tea, he charges seven or ten shillings, if he comes to wait at tea only he has five or seven shillings. If they had plenty to do in this way, it would be better than a trade. It's jeneraly done by servants out of place or servants that are set up in some buisness. I have eat of the good things until I am sick and now I am off to bed.

19th. Got up with a headache and feel stupid all day. Been out with the carriage this afternoon with Miss P. She kept me out longer than I thought she aught to of done, therefore I gave her a little row for it. I hope it will do her good. I served the old lady the same way the other day and it did her a deal of good, and I have no doubt it will act the same in this case …

June 23rd. Our people are beginning to talk of going out of London for a fiew weeks. I have been at home all day very buisy drawing.

29th … The old Lady has her last party today for this season and I am not sorry for it. I shall not have so much to do now, as there is no parteys nor no going out with the Carriage. In short, all my work comes easyer in the summer than it does in the winter. Felt very poorly. Have been to the doctor to get some physic. I hope it will do me good.

July 7th. We have been very buisy preparing to go to Brighton tomorrow. Plenty of packing up and runing about.

8th. Got up very early and of course very buisy loading the carriage … We started at half past ten [and] … arrived at Brighton at six o'clock, tired enough as the sun was enough to scorch us as we set outsid the carriage … We have a butifull view of the sea which comes almost up to the houses. We have a very nice house and very pleasently situated.

10th. Had a walk before breakfast. The sea air gives me an exolent apatite. The house has been thronged all day with tradespeople wanting to serve us with different things. I am going to sleep in one of the upper rooms which is much more airey and more healthey. Our family consists of Mrs and Miss P., and Mrs T.P. and Master W.P., three maid servants and myself.

11th. Have been this morning and had a bathe in the sea for the first time in my life. I like it very much. Have been walking about townd to make discoverys.

August 16th. [*Still at Brighton*] This day has been spent about the same as most of my others. The first thing I do in the morning is to get up at half past six, goes to the water's side, stays until eight, comes home, haves my breakfast, gets theirs ready at nine upstairs, then cleans the knives, fetches their breakfast down at ten, does a fiew other little jobs, and then goes out for a walk a little before eleven, and comes home a little before one. Gits their lunch ready and haves my own dinner by two, rests myself until three, then goes for a ride with the ladies until four, comes home, haves my tea, gets their dinner things ready at five, waits on them at dinner, brings it down and clears my part of it away by half past six, taks a walk or sits down and reads until eight, then takes up their tea, brings it down a little after eight, goes for another walk by the water's side for half an hour, then comes home and haves my supper. Goes to bed a little before eleven. In this way I goe on every day and so I mean to continue as long as I am here, as I shall not get such good air when I get to London, therefore I get all I can now. Very fiew servants go out so much as I do. Many have not an opertunity, some would rather stay at home and sleep, others would rather go to the publick house and get drunk, but I like pure air to either of this.

30th. Begining to pack up ready to start to London.

31st. Very buisy getting in bills and paying of them and wishing all our new acquaintance farwell.

September 1st. Up very early geting ready to be off. Wished good by to Brighton and started of at ten o'clock for London ...

30th. Had a strole in the Park before breakfast. I allways have my breakfast in the kitchen with the other servants now. Haveing a particular *friend* unwell [*his wife, who had given birth to their second son on 24th September*], I jenerally go to see her twice a day, that is, before dinner and before supper.

October 16th. Went out and paid a bill. The person gave me half a crown. Went and paid another where I only got sixpence, but I did not refuse it as I know two sixpences make a shilling.

22nd. Sunday is come once more. The weather continue very fine and much to dry for the farmers. I am got quite tired of this writeing as I do not improve as I expected I should, but I neglect writeing for two or three days sometimes, then I take up my pen and hurrey it over anyhow. I am a regular dunce and allways shall be ... We had company to dinner today.

November 15th. I received a note from G. Castle [*a cousin*] to inform me their butler was leaving his place and his master ofered him the place as upper servant and to be out of livery after a bit. George is the luckyest servant I ever heared of or know. No fellow can have tried to get on more than I have, but I cannot get on so fast as he does. He is very steady and well deserves all he has got ... If he gets this place which his master has promised him, he will not have such a very great catch. It will not be anear so profitable nor so comfortable as the one I have got. He will have a footman under him, which I have not; but if I have to do all the work, I have all the profits to myself, and there is no one about me, to see how I get them profits. When there are two men, a place cannot be made so profitable as where thear's only one. He and I started in service under very diferent advantages, he under the very best, and I under the very worst. I was four or five years in finding out the way of service, haveing no one to show me, and I taught him the whole art of service in one year or less, as I took an interest and pleasure in showing him everything I could.

December 4th. I have been in this place three years today all but *three months*. Therefore this is my rent day, the day on which I take my wages. We are payed every quarter. I get ten pound, ten shillings a quarter. That is forty two pounds pr. year, my victuals and drink and lodgings in the bargan, besides all the perqusites I can make in such services as mine. These perquasites jenerally amount to about ten or fifteen pounds pr. year more or less, but it's more frequently very much less as service is getting very bad buisness.

26th. This is what is called about here Boxing Day. It's the day the people goe from house to house gathering their Christmas boxes. We have had numbers here today – sweeps, beadles, lamplighters, watermen, dutsmen, scavengers ... newspaper boy, general postmen, twopenny postmen ... All these people expect to have a shilling or half a crown each ... Miss P. gave me half a sovering for a Christmas box, one of the trades people gave me half a crown, another gave me a shilling. I mite get fuddled two or three times a day if I had a mind, as all the trades people that serve this house are very pressing with their glass of something to drink their health this Christmas time.

30th. The life of a gentleman's servant is something like that of a bird shut up in a cage. The bird is well housed and well fed but is deprived of liberty, and liberty is the dearest and sweetes object of all Englishmen ... I would rather be like the sparrow or lark, have less houseing and feeding and rather more liberty. A servant is shut up like a bird in a cage, deprived of the benefit of the air to the very great ingurey of the constitution. In London, men servants has to sleep down stairs underground, which is jeneraly very damp. Many men loose their lives by it or otherwise eat up with the rhumatics. One mite see fine blooming young men come from the country to take services, but after they have been in London one year, all the bloom is lost and a pale yellow sickley complexion in its stead. There is money to be made in service, but the person must be luckey enough to get in good places and begin service when very young. I was very much to old when I began service, therefore I never shall be worth a jot. If a person wish to see life, I would advise them to be a gentleman's servant. They will see high life and low life, above stairs as well as life below. They will see and know more than any other class of people in the world.

William and his wife Maria had four children. In later life, William became a butler; he died in 1892.

Hannah Cullwick

Maidservant, Scullion and Pot-girl

Hannah Cullwick worked all her life in domestic service and her unique diaries were written at the behest of Arthur Munby, the man who later became her husband. This extract comes from 'Hannah's Places', originally published in *The Diaries of Hannah Cullwick: Victorian Maidservant* edited by Liz Stanley (Virago Press, 1984). It is reproduced by the kind permission of Liz Stanley and Virago Press. Here, Hannah describes her employers, the nature of her work and how she found her different jobs through servants' registries, personal recommendations and newspapers.

Hannah's places ... from her leaving the Charity school in Shifnal, which was at eight year old ... a friend of Mother's (Mrs Phillips) took me to work at her house off & on (not hired) from 1841 to about 43 ...

And might glad I was for going to Mrs Phillips, for the living which was good & strenthen'd me, as I was growing fast & tall & 'cause Mrs P. was so very kind to me & teach'd me how to do everything properly – to wait at table, to wash up, to clean silver, & indeed everything. So, as she said, there wasn't a job I couldn't do as well as the cook or housemaid could. She always prais'd me after I'd clean'd the red brick floor on my hands & knees & scour'd the big white tables in the kitchen. And I could clean the dining room & the bright long hall, & the door steps & all before breakfast. The Missis always said I sh'd be her servant when I was old enough & I could sew neatly at Irish cloth shirts or shifts, so I did that too. Mrs P. used to take me with her for a ride, or a fishing, & I carried the stool & mind'd the little dog. At last I wasn't wanted & the Master gave me a *sovereign*, & I jump'd for joy, & looked at it as such a prize, but I was going to live at home again getting nothing after I'd once began ...

I got a place at the Lion for a shilling a week & stopp'd eight months. There I clean'd the tables & floors & even waited on the farmers dinner of a market day. They gave me always 2^D or a penny each on the plate as I carried round o'purpose, after the cheese, making a curtsy to them as give the most, 'cause I thought they was the biggest farmers. But my father thought it wasn't good for me there at a public house & I was to give warning.

[*Hannah went to work for Mrs Phillips again.*]

At last my kind Missis died. I'd bin there entirely twelve months, slept in the house & all. She kept her bed & she had me to wait on her & all I could, & gave me a lot of her things for she was sure of dying … It was in July 1847 when she died & I'd a suit o'black & follow'd her to the grave. In Sept or early in Oct I got the nursery-maid's place at Ryton & went to it. A month after my mother came to see me, & in December both my father & her was dead. So I never saw them again, for they died of a fever just a fortnight 'twixt each other & my Missis wouldn't let me go …

I stopp'd here through the winter & had a deal of hard work to do, for there was eight children. I'd all their boots to clean & the large nurseries on my hands & knees, & a long passage & stairs, all their meals to get & our own – the nurse only dress'd the baby & look'd over me. I'd all the water to carry up & down for their baths & coal for the fire, put all the children to bed & wash & dress of a morning by eight, & I wasn't in bed after 5. But what I couldn't bear was the Missis rushing at me as she did with wild-looking eyes, & I told my aunt it was very uncomfortable & she told me to leave.

[*Hannah then went to work at her aunt's farm.*]

Before the year was out I heard of a place at Newport to be nurserymaid to 5 children at a lawyer's & a biggish house. I went after the place & got it at 5 lbs [£5] a year. I come in July or August, stay'd 15 months. And in the next summer I was took to the seaside – to Southport, a long ride & a wonderful thing I thought it & very good luck.

In 1849 I left to go into Lincolnshire to a clergyman's where I was to have 8 lbs [£8] a year & a better place. My cousin had just left it & they tried me. This family was very particular & the young gentleman (Master Scotsman) used to correct me often in talk. I learned a good deal from them & I was there 15 months. But I was too young for that place, only the lady kept me on a bit, & she was very kind & give me a good character to Lady Boughy of Aqualate Hall.

I came there in 1850 & I was 17 years old in the May. I got on very well as under housemaid for eight months, but Lady Boughy saw me & another playing as we was cleaning our kettles (we had about 16 to clean, they belong'd to the bedrooms) & she gave us both warning. Then I heard a scullion was wanted under a man cook at Woodcote [*Hall, near Shifnal*] & I went after the place. Mind I was dreadfully sorry to leave that splendid park at Aqualate. I was got used to the servants & I felt happy for I had a friend or two, & John the postillion was such a good-looking little fellow & used to take me for a walk in the park with Mary Hart, a nice girl and kind to me ...

[*Lady Boughy*] gave me a good character to Lady Louisa Cotes & I went there, into the scullery. It was very different work, & a very different place to me after being used to running along the splendid halls & gallery & rooms at Aqualate as a housemaid. And I had learnt to make beds & to do the rooms there for company & all, so that I couldn't help crying when I came to clean the stew pans & great spits & dripping pan, & live only in a rough outhouse next to the kitchen, & could only get out through the coalhole *unseen*, with no windows to look out for anything. But I got used to it, & I used to run over to Aqualate (about 3 miles) of a Sunday afternoon & Jim would come back with me. I liked him for company but I didn't ever want him for a sweetheart ... My fellow servants ... teased me about him. I knew I was too young for a sweetheart so I didn't mind them ...

Well, in the autumn the family went to Rhyl & left the cook & me in the home & took the kitchenmaid. I had servants' dinner to get ready & wash up & that. In the evening the housekeeper told me to go & help the housemaids. I did it some days, & when my master the cook came to know it he told me not to go. He said I'd enough dirty hard work to do when the family was at home, & I was to go out for walks, if I'd any spare time, so I did. But I felt lonely & I began to wish I had somebody to love me again ... But the time soon went by & the family came back, company came to stop, & then the winter with all the business as there *is* in a big family, & I forgot I was lonely.

The Lady's father Lord Liverpool died & in the following spring the family went to London. What was the most delightful news I could hear was that I was to go with the cook – the kitchenmaid was to be left to go to Pitchford [*the family's second home in Shropshire*] with the children. I was 18 years old this May 1851 & I'd orders to get ready for going to London in April. We went to Lower Brook St, Grosvenor Square, hired of Col. Hutchinson for two months. I was pleas'd with London, & besides, I was more at work in the kitchen & I thought it better for me to *learn* more.

In '51, I'd orders to go again next to 12 Grosvenor Street. I was still scullion but the cook said I was a good 'un to work & he'd rather have me nor Emma the kitchen-maid. I came back again at the end of two months, with the family, to Pitchford again & from there to Woodcote for the two grand balls at Shrewsbury. The company stay'd at Pitchford for them, so we was both very gay & hard-work'd too, for I seem'd as pleas'd to peep through the bushes to see the ladies & gentlemen start as if I was one of 'em.

[In May 1854, when she was still working for the family during one of their London stays, Hannah met her future husband Arthur Munby, an author, poet and barrister, when he spoke to her in the street. Her choice of subsequent places in service was often influenced by wanting to be nearer to him; she called him 'Massa'.]

I was to leave London again wi' the family in June – I come back early in '55. I had to leave Woodcote. I started to London & got lodgings, in the *cold*, a tiny room it was, for 5 & 6^D a week. There Massa came to see me again …

At the end of three weeks I got another kitchenmaid's place … at Lord Shadbroke's. But it was at Henham in Suffolk, a long way off, & I shall never forget how miserable I felt when M. wish'd me goodbye & left me alone ready to start at 5 o'clock next morning. I rode to Shoreditch station & then had a cold ride in the train to Ipswich. After that 30 miles in the coach to the Lodge gates where the laundrymaid met me with a man & a cart for my box … Mrs Smith the housekeeper was most unkind to me in ordering & I was ready to say I'd go back in the morning. I told Bill the groom I would but he said, 'Never mind her, she's drunk & doesn't know what she's about – you stop & you'll get on all right,' & as it was winter & so far back I thought I'd try to stop. The scullion had gone with the kitchen maid but another was got. Mrs Smith gave up coming in the kitchen after 2 or 3 months …

In the spring, for the first time, my lord went to a house in London & took the butler & a footman, a housemaid & *me*, for two months. I shall never forget how delighted I felt when Mary Clark the housemaid whisper'd to me what she believed – that a house was took & that I sh'd have to go as well as her. I thought I *was* lucky after all, & I sh'd see my Massa again.

Well, we … started early one fine morning. The butler rode in the same carriage with us & talk'd quite freely & joked with us but I was thinking mostly of who I sh'd see when I got to London. It was a nice little house in South St, Park Lane, & there I had to wait on the butler & the town housekeeper & clean their sitting room, do the front steps & all the lowest places underground. But I liked the work & Massa used to come up 2 or 3 times a week & go in the park with me. And when I could I ax'd leave for the evening & went to the Temple with him – for M. had shown me the way & ax'd me to go, *if I liked*. Of course I was shy at it first, but I wasn't *afraid* …

The time come again & I went back to Henham again. I ax'd the housekeeper Mrs Smith if she would speak to L. Shadbroke for my young sister Ellen to be scullerymaid with me. He spoke with me … & he said my sister might come. I sent money for her to get clothes, & on a *Friday* about August she came, 1855 … Soon after we went to Woodcote again. My sister was with me in the winter at Henham & we was order'd again to London in the spring, & I didn't go back again. Massa came to see me in Suffolk & lost his way on the road back to his hotel in Halesworth, & he told me if I stopp'd then he wouldn't come again.

And then I got a place out 'o the newspaper, at a Jew's family in Westhame Park. I lik'd the place for some things – the work was regular & I was a proper maid of all work like except waiting at table. I clean'd the knives & boots, the doorsteps & all that, & I was content at 16 lbs [£16] a year. But a fresh housemaid came, named Ellen [who] wasn't satisfied with her new place & besides that she knew of a couple just married & on their tour for a month as wanted two servants; the sister was to engage 'em. So E. went & got the place as housemaid & the parlourmaid, me to go after the general servant's place.

So I went & the lady liked me & I was hired again at 16 lbs [£16] a year. My Missis didn't like me leaving so soon, but I got away a fortnight after & went to my new place of a *Saturday* in August 1856, & stopp'd through '57–58, '59–60 & left just before Good Friday 1861, being there 4 years & a ½. It was at a Mr and Mrs Jackson's & we had a nice place for 3 years, but the family got bigger & Mr J. came poorer through extravagance & had to leave his business at the upholstering & went to live at Haslington. It was too far off. My Master & I wanted to leave, & I'd got a place opposite at Mr Foster's, the beer merchants ...

I soon got at home with the other servants ... I had the Master's & young gentlemen's boots to clean there, the breakfast to lay & wait on & to wash up after. I found it hard. So much to get ready as well as the cleaning, but I stopp'd for 3 years there & they took us all to Brighton for 2 months every year. At last Miss Louisa kept the breakfast about late & I couldn't stop to turn my sleeves down every time I went up, & I couldn't get the things away afore it was dinner time. And it was too much work altogether with so much company, & that as the Missis said, I'd better leave & I did. I was sorry for a good many things. I got good wages & I could be sure of every Sunday evening to see M. Still it was too much & I felt overpower'd & Massa thought it'd be good for me to go to Margate for a change.

It was 3 years on this Good Friday 1864, & there was a cheap train to Margate. I hardly liked the thought o' going alone but however I did ... I got up at 5 next morning & started with my bag & bundle & reach'd Margate by 12. The woman I ax'd for lodgings took me to her house, but she didn't care to keep me on but took me to another place where I got friendly wi' the Missis. [I] used to do anything – help her to wash & nail up the curtains, help the man with the 'tatoes, or *anything*, for I couldn't bear to sit sewing or walking out alone.

And after a while I call'd at a Register office & put my name in for a job. One day after that (I was dress'd in my cotton frock & apron & cap as usual) a person come & ax'd [for] me. Although she was so plainly dress'd the minute I saw her & heard her speak I could tell she was a lady, so I curtsied. And she ax'd me if I wanted a place. I told her how I didn't care what it was as I was only come for a change & wanted to fill my time up at work. So she said what her place was – a general servant. And I took it *weekly*. At 4 shillings I think, but it was at the rate of 12 lbs [£12] a year & at a lodging house or boarding house, which is the same nearly except that the meals are [taken] together. The house was dirty, having had no servant nor lodgers hardly through winter. But there *was* one now & Miss Knight & her sister, one an invalid & always upstairs, & daughters of an officer, couldn't do without a servant. I waited on them & the lodgers & fill'd my time up wi' cleaning the house down, & the windows. And I took the blinds all down & wash'd 'em, ironed & starch'd 'em & put 'em up again. I liked being alone in the kitchen, & my work, & the air at Margate, & used to go to church, & [I] could write freely & nicely that I felt quite happy ...

I used to clean the grates with my hands before the Miss Knights. [I] scrubbed away till I was all of a sweat, & I used my hands all I could – to shove the soot & cinders up & all that. A good deal of rough work I got through there ... They was ladies, but poor through their having a second mother, so they kept this for a living. I was sorry when I left in October, but they couldn't afford to keep me when the lodgers was gone, & I wanted too to get nearer Massa again ...

When I come back to London I went to the Servants' Home near the Strand. M. found he mustn't stop in town his head ach'd so bad [*he had been thrown off his horse*], & I heard of a place at St Leonards through the Matron & took it. Miss Knight gave me a capital character & I'd got Mrs Foster's too so I sent both. Mrs Caulfield hired me from them & the Matron's good word, & I went just at Christmas time & stopp'd two years.

I had 5 fireplaces to do at Mrs Caulfield's every morning, the dining room & study & the halls & steps, the lady's maid's room & all the places on the lower ground to keep clean. There was a nice garden to look at & they went away twice for two months, leaving us servants our board wages, which was very nice & we could do as we liked & that while they was away. It was a real gentleman's family. We had plenty o' work while they was at home & when they was out we cleaned the house thoroughly all throughout, & I worked in the garden if I liked. But I was so far off Massa & at last I give notice & I left.

[At] the end of 1867, [I] come to London & went to the Soho Bazaar [*a servants' registry office*] & got a place at another lodging house in Craven Street,

Charing Cross, at a Mrs Bishops ... [I] stopp'd only 3 months, for Mrs Bishop was a vulgar person & couldn't understand me. She kept a private hotel & boarding house & took in lodgers. I saw that she was vulgar at the bazaar & I oughtn't to o' took the place. But it was near to Massa, & Mrs Bishop spoke fair about wages & letting me go out so I thought I might do ... I was to get all the meals ready, keep coffee & boiling water always ready, clean the hall & steps every morning, the stairs & kitchen, pantry, larder & scullery, & to clean the boots & knives if there was only a few lodgers. I did all I could to show that I liked dirty hard work, but Mrs Bishop never seemed satisfied, & I wasn't either. There was a something about the place so low lifed, & yet I thought I needn't mind so long as I could work on & be honest & get out to see Massa easily. But the Missis said I didn't look after her interests enough in the board & things for the lodgers, so she give me warning after two months & it was well ...

I left again & ... then I went to a register office & paid ½ a crown. The gentleman got me a place at an asylum in the country & the lady was satisfied with my character & I nearly settled when to go, but Massa seem'd inclin'd for me to go to Miss Knight's at Margate again & I wrote to her. [*Hannah returned to Margate to work for Miss Knight during the summer.*]

When I left Margate, I went to the bazaar [in London] & hired myself to Mrs Redmayne of Gloucester Gardens but I wasn't wanted till January ... I found plenty of work but at the end of three months, March 1868, I'd warning to leave *there* for the master was order'd abroad & we *all* had to leave. I had a hard place but I was vex'd at having to leave so soon. Next I was egg'd on to go after a better sort o' place at Mrs Sanders where a kitchenmaid was kept. I walk'd up & down & look'd at the house, afraid to go in. But I went & saw Mrs Sanders & she seem'd to like me, & was quite willing to try me, & I was to have high wages – *22 lbs* [£22]. They got my character & I went in April 1868.

They was going in the country to live in the Isle O' Wight & I was going with 'em but something happened that stopp'd it. The manservant was prying & got to know who I wrote to, & this man had lived [as a] servant at a relation of Massa's & waited on him, so that he know'd him quite well. M. walk'd pass'd one Sunday waiting for me, & this man saw him & made the worst of it to Mr Sanders & he ax'd me about it. I told him it was true, but no harm in it, Mr Sanders said he quite believed me, but he couldn't let me stop after so much was know'd. And I said it was much better too, 'cause the servants would think bad of it. Besides I didn't feel fit to have a kitchenmaid under me, 'cause I wanted to do the washing up & the roughest work myself. So I left & I got a place again as general servant where a housemaid & a boy was kept.

Hannah stayed in this new place working for Mrs Henderson until late February 1872, followed by a few more short-term charring jobs. She married Arthur Munby on 3 January 1873 and lived with him at the Temple, the Inns of Court on the Embankment in London, working as his servant and housekeeper, until October 1877 when she returned to Shropshire. Their relationship was complex and although they mostly lived apart, Munby visited Hannah regularly and their marriage lasted until her death in 1909.

Part II

1850–1900

The 'Servant Problem'

Mistresses lament over the want of good servants, and servants protest against the domination of mistresses. The two classes survey each other like the ranks of opposing armies; and the feeling of hostility grows with rank luxuriance until most unfortunately quite a wrong spirit is engendered between them; and the mistress takes the servant into her house as if she were something to be suspected; while the servant views a situation with the same feeling with which an intelligent but unfortunate fly may be supposed to regard a spider's web.

(*Hampshire Advertiser*, 10 September 1892)

The 'servant problem' was the complaint vociferously made by employers that they could not get good servants or struggled to retain them. Contemporary newspapers printed column after column of correspondence and opinion pieces about this perceived predicament, but the argument rumbled on.

In the 1850s and 1860s, when the middle classes started employing servants in large numbers, maids were inexpensive and the supply of potential staff ample. Employers' objections at this stage were about the quality of their domestic staff, not their scarcity. Later in the century, it was no coincidence that the 'servant problem' was experienced most acutely by the middle-classes (many lower middle-class mistresses had been servants themselves), nor that reports of it coincided with a gradual change in the relationship between servant and mistress.

Throughout the eighteenth century and the first half of the nineteenth, servants in smaller households had a more familial standing. They were considered part of the family, and the daughters of the household might assist them in daily chores, such as baking and dusting. The Victorian middle classes, however, wanted to ape the gentry and sought to enforce social segregation below stairs. In a household employing just one servant, this could mean forcing the maid to eat all her meals alone in the kitchen and having no social contact with her whatsoever.

One young servant's experience of this disorientating situation was recounted in an article, 'Maids of all Work', published in the *Cornhill Magazine* in 1874. She had been brought up in a workhouse and went into service at thirteen: 'I cried the first night ... I had always slept in a ward full of other girls, and there I was all alone, and this was a great big house – oh, so big, and they told me to go downstairs, in a room by the kitchen all alone, with a long black passage. I might have screamed, but nobody would have heard.'

The 'servant problem' was being debated as early as 1862, by writers such as Harriet Martineau, who produced an article for the *Edinburgh Review*, entitled 'Modern Domestic Service'. She commented on the decreasing allure of domestic service for working-class people:

> *public opinion among the class at the present time is in favour of the independence of factory and other day-work: and this explains the difficulty of the existing case of domestic service. In one word it is independence against dependence ... Service is becoming a mere contract for wages; the moral dignity of the condition is departing; and contract for contract, that which leaves a man the largest amount of freedom and the largest profits becomes the most attractive.*

Alternative Employment

Part of the 'servant problem' was attributed to the increasingly wide range of employment opportunities for the working-class girls who had traditionally gone into domestic service. Factories were particularly attractive, especially after working hours were limited under the Factory Acts. From 1878, women were to work for no more than 56 hours a week, and unlike a servant, the factory girl's leisure time was her own – she was not constantly at the beck and call of her employer. Shop work was also popular for the same reasons. The desire for independence exerted a strong influence because financially, factory and shop girls were often worse off; they had to pay for their own food and lodgings out of their wages, whereas indoor domestic servants usually had everything provided for them. This was a point alluded to in a report written by C. V. Butler for the Government just before the First World War. It noted 'the most promising girls are apt to prefer lower wages, less material comfort, and much less security of employment in shop or office or factory work, to the often-quoted advantages of domestic service.'

After 1880, working-class girls were educated for longer and to a higher standard, and their view of the world and their own place within it was widened as a result. The most intelligent could now aspire to enter professions like teaching and nursing in greater numbers, while clerical work offered further opportunities away from domestic service.

By the end of the nineteenth century, the scarcity of servants became a talking point, rather than their alleged inadequacies. The *Blackburn Standard* (15 April 1899) reported that in London, around 60,000 girls were employed in milliners and dress shops; more than 15,000 were engaged in hospital and infirmary nursing; while over 3,000 girls were employed in tea shops and restaurants run by large companies such as Lyons and the Aerated Bread Company. Working in a post-office was also attractive to girls who would have been servants in former decades. In 1899, the Post Office in London employed 17,463 'non-established female staff for whose services no very high standard of education is necessary', plus upwards of 13,000 head and sub-postmistresses.

'No followers'

The late Victorian trend among the working classes to turn away from domestic service was inextricably linked with the relationship between mistress and maid. According to Harriet Martineau, servants were 'cruelly dependent on the temper and notions of their employers', and it made no difference whether they were housemaids, scullery maids, lady's maids or footmen.

On entering the service of a new employer, the domestic servant was expected to adhere to a long list of household rules or risk being dismissed without a character. Young girls from the countryside found this especially hard; they had usually come from lively homes with plenty of company from siblings and childhood friends, and they were used to an outdoor life with plenty of fresh air.

Their lives in service were summed up by journalist Eliza Lynn Linton in 'On the Side of the Maids', (*Cornhill Magazine*, 29, 1874):

No followers, no friends in the kitchen, no laughing to be heard above stairs, no romping for young girls to whom romping is an instinct all the same as with lambs and kittens, no cessation of work save at meal-times, no getting out for half an hour into the bright sunshine, save "on the sly," or after the not always pleasant process of asking leave; and above all, education for the fancy or the intellect beyond a dull magazine for Sunday reading, which is held quite sufficient recreation for lonely Betty moping in the dreary kitchen on the afternoon of her Sunday in.

In the eighteenth and early nineteenth centuries, very few servants had any formally recognised time off, except for church attendance. By the 1890s, it became more common for them to have at least one day off a month, plus a weekday evening and some time on Sunday. In fact, days off and holidays began to be used as inducements to attract good servants, especially by smaller households employing one or two maids, where high wages could not be offered. Clara Collet's *Report on the Money Wages of Indoor Domestic Servants* (1899) discovered that when granting holidays to their servants, these mistresses often suffered a 'much greater personal inconvenience', because the work had to be 'performed by the mistress or her family or by a charwoman requiring extra pay.'

The growing fashion for Sunday entertaining adversely affected servants, because they were expected to forego their afternoon off (if it was usually given on Sundays) in order to work instead. The Sabbath was never a day of rest for them.

Writing in *Englishwoman's Review* (1873), Jessie Boucherett compared the working hours of housemaids, factory girls and shopwomen and concluded that the housemaid worked the hardest. She broke down the average housemaid's working hours as follows:

> *A housemaid is usually required to begin work soon after six o'clock am and goes to bed after ten pm. She has for rest, half an hour for breakfast, an hour for dinner, and half an hour each for tea and supper, in all two hours and a half for meals, and in the afternoon she is generally required to do needlework for an hour and a half, which may fairly be regarded as rest, giving altogether four hours' rest. This leaves twelve hours of actual work, longer by two hours than the day's work of factory women, and longer than the usual day's work of a shopwoman.*

The housemaid's work was also more strenuous than that of the factory girl, because she had to carry loads of coal and water, and to lift heavy weights while making beds and emptying baths. She had more limited leisure time, compared with the factory girl and shopwoman's complete day off each week. Mondays were particularly arduous in families where the washing was done at home, as the maid was 'often required to rise at three or four in the morning to help the laundry-maid.'

To put this into perspective, Jessie Boucherett commented, 'it is well known that a housemaid's work is considered lighter than that of a cook, kitchen-maid, scullery maid, or dairymaid.' What Boucherett does not point out is that the times she specifies for 'rest' would have been constantly interrupted by the sound of the wire-operated bells in use from the Georgian period onward. These were extremely convenient for the employer, because they allowed for total segregation of the servants' quarters from those of the family and meant that maids could be called to any area of the house at any time.

Servants' living quarters differed dramatically between households, but maids' bedrooms were frequently situated high up in the attics, which made them freezing cold in winter and unbearably hot in summer. Where more than one servant was kept, they often had to share a room, even if they did not get on well together. This was, however, preferable to having to sleep on a fold-down bed in a damp, dark, beetle-infested basement kitchen, which was the lot of many a single-handed 'general' working in a tradesmen's household. Even in larger, wealthier townhouses where footmen were employed, male servants were obliged to sleep in the basement to ensure segregation of the sexes.

The phrase 'wages not so much an object as comfortable home' was commonly used from the 1880s in 'Situations Wanted' advertisements placed by servants. For older female servants, especially those for whom marriage was no longer an option, favourable conditions were more important than a high salary.

In addition to the long hours of drudgery, employers subjected their servants to loneliness by severely restricting the number and gender of friends they could invite into the kitchen. Unless special arrangements had been agreed, 'no followers' were allowed by most households, which meant that if a female servant was 'keeping company', then she could not invite her sweetheart to the house to see her. Opportunities for courtship were extremely limited and similar rules applied to female friends or relatives, leaving servants cut off from their former companions. In a large household with lots of staff, this may not have been such a problem as there was often a great deal of camaraderie; they also had more opportunities for servants' outings and parties.

To solve the problem of followers, Elizabeth Banks in *Campaigns of Curiosity* (1894) suggested that servants have:

> *the use of a comfortable sitting-room, where they may receive visitors on certain afternoons or evenings, the number of their callers and the length of their stay being kept, of course, within the bounds of reason. The present class of servant-girls have much cause for complaint on this score. To stipulate that a girl shall have no visitors is as unkind as it is unreasonable and dangerous. A young woman servant is quite likely to have friends of both sexes, and it is probable that she is*

"keeping company". To compel her future husband to hang over the area-fence whistling for her to come out, or to oblige her to go to the park and sit on the benches in order to have a talk with him, is not only inconsiderate, it is almost indecent. She should be allowed to receive him once a week or once a fortnight in the servant's hall. It is not difficult to arrange this matter satisfactorily if reason is shown on the part of both employer and employed.

There is no doubt that servants were at risk of sexual exploitation by their employers and visitors to the household, as well as other members of staff. It is difficult to know how widespread the problem was, but both male and female staff had no right to privacy; they could not lock their bedroom doors, so it is easy to see how unwanted sexual advances could be made.

The records of the Foundling Hospital in London provide detailed information about how applicants wanting to leave their babies in the care of the institution came to be seduced. A large number were servants and, in *Love in the Time of Victoria: Sexuality, Class and Gender in Nineteenth-Century London*, Françoise Barret-Ducrocq quotes the story of Mary Ann, a maid of all work for a wheelwright in Camberwell. Within six weeks of starting work, Mary Ann's master had started making sexual advances towards her, but, as Barret-Ducrocq reveals, when she complained to her mistress, her only response was to call her 'a ninny, a flirt and a scatterbrain. A few months later, after a short struggle, she was raped by her master in the kitchen.'

In her statement to the Foundling Hospital committee, Mary Ann gave more details about the attack: 'Mrs P. was at the Queens Theatre and went home at night. I told Mrs P the next morning but she pretended not to believe it … It was repeated when Mrs P was at Church, also by force and Father [her master] said he would give me some medicine if I fell in the family way. I left the P's and went to my mothers [sic].' Although Mary Ann made an official complaint, nothing could be done before the child was born, by which time the wheelwright and his wife had disappeared. Mary Ann was apparently not the first servant Mr P had 'got into trouble'.

If a female servant became pregnant, the sexual double standard prevalent in Victorian society came into play. Many employers would ask her to leave immediately, although more charitable mistresses might arrange for maternity care and even to have the child adopted. However, similar punishment was rarely meted out to the father, if he was known to be a member of staff. If she had no family to turn to, then her future was bleak, and once her savings ran out, she had little choice but to enter the workhouse. Many desperate servants tried to end their pregnancies, and some took the difficult decision to place their children in the care of a charity, such as the Foundling Hospital in London.

Servants' Grievances

The correspondence columns of daily newspapers were among the few places where servants could publicly air their complaints against employers. Their letters are frequently well argued, intelligent and heart-felt, and demonstrate a high level of literacy, indicative of increasing access to education. The *Western Mail* (29 November 1892) printed a request from 'A Servant' of Swansea for 'protection against tyrannous mistresses':

Will you insert a servant's complaints of the way in which the majority of that much-abused class are treated? No one seems to heed our long hours or our holidays, which are (like angels' visits) few and far between. There seems no other class working at a greater disadvantage. For instance, no servant can expect a situation who had not got a good reference and a long one from where she last lived. It often happens she has been living with unprincipled people, who think not half so much of their servants as they do of their dumb animals. What is it to them if the girl does not get a situation? She has offended them in some way or other. Perhaps she had had more than her share of work, bad food, and other things too numerous to mention, and she has spoken too plainly to please them. That, of course, is considered impertinent, for, according to many mistresses' opinion, a servant is a being made expressly for them, and she has no rights whatever, and she is told she need not expect a character. What are servants to do under these circumstances? They may be out of a situation for months – perhaps something worse. Do the mistresses think we have no spirit, and that we must bear quietly the petty tyranny they have it in their power to use in a hundred ways? My two last situations have happened to be places where it is impossible for servants to live, I being the sixth servant in three months, and yet we have nothing and no one to warn us of places of this sort. I think it is a serious matter that our character (I may say our livelihood) is at the mercy of such people. Why cannot something be done to benefit servants as well as other working classes? Servants ought to know what kind of places they are going into, as well as the character of the people they are to live with.

The Swansea woman's letter is typical of those written by servants to protest against ill-treatment. In the days that followed, other maids wrote to the *Western*

Mail listing their own problems with their employers. 'A Poor Servant in Pembrokeshire' added:

> *I am only grieved to say that we servants are worse treated than pet animals. They are studied with fresh air every day, but we do not need it once a week even. Are we allowed sufficient time to eat the food we get, which would not be often given to their pets? When we enter into an engagement with a lady we are asked if we can obtain a good character. Should there be a little spot, "Oh you won't suit me." Should the lady's character be inquired into as closely as the servant's, I wonder which would prove the most just. You are asked if you are honest. Is it needed where everything is locked. You are expected to be clean. Can you be clean in some 'houses' where you have a piece of soap locked from you?*

Lack of trust between mistress and maid was a constant source of frustration and anger. Employers also wrote in to the *Western Mail* to have their say during this discussion. 'A Mistress' of Park-place, Cardiff commented:

> *I do not doubt that among servants, like every other class, there are some who are badly treated, but ... what of the gross carelessness and wicked wastefulness of servants, and what of their growing antipathy to doing the ordinary work of a household? Servants, nowadays, are not to be compared to the honest and industrious worker of a few years ago, and their grievances are entirely of their own making.*

This letter provoked an impassioned reply from 'A Servant' of Newport, who wrote in response:

> *I have heard many say that modern servants are not like the old-fashioned ones, but mistresses of the present day are very different from what they were then. Mistresses used to respect their servants and were looked up to in return, but such mistresses now are few and far between. There are so many 'ladies' who have been domestics themselves that we cannot expect them to make good mistresses. I should think that to have a good place we should have a kind mistress. This is the chief thing; then the girl would find it a pleasure to be industrious.*

A butler with 17 years' experience wrote:

I respectfully contend that servants are far more honest now than they were years ago, when many of them had little or no wages more than their food. No, servants are not what they were years ago. They, like other branches of the community, have improved with the times, and are still improving. But why is it they meet with so little encouragement from their employers? Hundreds of societies are formed, recreation-rooms built, and everything conceivable is done for the improvement of the clerk, artisan, mechanic, &c. Mistresses subscribe liberally to any of these, but no helping hand is held out to the poor being who is unlucky enough to bear the insignificant designation of "servant" ... I am happy to say from experience that there are some few mistresses who take an interest in their servants, and do all they possibly can to encourage them to be thrifty &c, and improve themselves, not only by giving them good advice, but with kind, substantial help. But while employers continue to treat servants as machines, expecting all and giving as little as possible in return (for it is not solely a question of wages), there will be a difficulty in obtaining good servants.

From an employer calling herself 'Queen-Street' came this nugget of common sense: 'I have always found that if you are kind and considerate towards servants they, too, will do their duty towards you, and probably more. I may add that we keep three servants, of whom the cook has been here eight years, the parlour-maid fourteen years, and the page-boy three years and a half.'

Finally came the hopes of 'A Cardiff Girl':

Would you kindly allow me a small space in your valuable paper to refer to the proposed servants' union. I am sorry to see that such a few girls of this town have taken the matter up. Why do not some of them come forward with pluck and energy and stand out one with the other until they get a union like the shop assistants and have a half-holiday once a week, with some part of the day on Sunday, instead of being penned in like prisoners once a fortnight? I am sure we deserve it, I sincerely hope, now the girls have made a stir that it will not result in a failure like the last.

Servants' Trade Unions

The reference by 'A Cardiff Girl' to the 'failure' to form a servants' union is indicative of the fact that trade unionism had very little influence on the lot of domestic servants. There had been unsuccessful attempts to set up servants' unions in Leamington and Dundee in 1872, and in 1891, the London and

Provincial Domestic Servants' Union was founded, with goals such as making it compulsory by law for all employers 'to give a true and just character in writing to servants on leaving their employ'.

The new union also wanted to bring servants' registry office keepers under official supervision; to increase the rate of wages and number of hours for necessary outdoor recreation, especially on Sundays; to establish union homes in all districts of London and provincial towns, where good living accommodation could be obtained at moderate charges; and to establish registry offices in connection with the union homes. However, it was difficult to recruit members – even at its peak, there were less than 600 servants in the union – and it was finally dissolved in 1898.

The main problem the union had encountered in recruiting members was that, unlike other industries, most domestic service workers were employed in small households, not in large-scale operations; this made it more difficult to conduct recruitment drives. The contract between servant and their employer was a private one, and maids ran the risk of being blacklisted if they were discovered to be members of a union.

Remedies for the 'Servant Problem'

Over the years, a number of novel ideas were put forward to solve the 'servant problem', some serious, others less so. *The Times* (25 July 1899) ran an advertisement for one London householder who proposed employing Chinese servants in 50 households, 'to reduce the expenses of agency in China, passages, &c.' He stressed that 'Chinamen' were known to make good servants because they were 'civil, honest, sober, reliable and invariably good cooks.' No further reference was made to the experiment.

Another quirky idea was to employ men as housemaids, as one London manufacturer apparently did (*Daily Gazette for Middlesbrough*, 20 March 1897). Having received hundreds of applications for a vacant clerkship while his wife could not get a satisfactory 'general', he suggested, half-jokingly, to one candidate that:

> he might try his hand at the feminine work rather than do nothing ... The mistress was induced to give the new "maid" a week's trial, and despite the sneers of other servants the brave young man (being adaptive and willing) soon learnt sufficient to make a most efficient substitute. He has no pride, he says, and he does not care a whit if seen whitening the doorsteps or cleaning

the windows. He ... does all the usual duties of a general servant. With a civil tongue and tact rather above the average maid's, he is getting more than he would earn as a junior clerk; while the employer and his wife are recommending the new idea to their friends as a brilliant solution of the "servant difficulty".

Various enterprises also attempted to address the issue of training young servants correctly. One such scheme was reported by the *Berwickshire News and General Advertiser* (19 January 1892) at Lady Humphrey's house in Cambridge. All the work of the house was carried out by around six or eight little maids, aged from 12 to 15, who learned 'in turn the duties of housemaid, parlourmaid and cook etc.' The girls stayed for little more than a year in her house, and were then sent out to other situations. Lady Humphrey took the girls in from deprived homes, subjecting them to 'the influence of an orderly and systematic household. The trained maids, assisted by the mistress, teach the new girl one kind of work at a time.' Although successful on a small scale, such schemes could not hope to make a difference for the majority of embattled maids and mistresses.

In the 1870s, Mrs Crawshay's 'lady helps' were proposed as another remedy. Under the scheme, which she introduced in her home at Cyfartha Castle, Merthyr Tydfil, gentlewomen who had fallen on hard times were encouraged to go into domestic service as 'upper servants'. The idea did not really catch on, largely because of the difficulty in maintaining social distinction between 'lady helps' and ordinary servants, and the reluctance of gentlewomen to 'lower themselves'.

In 1892, a new organisation called The Household Auxiliary Association announced that it would send 'ladies' into service. According to their literature, these women were 'not to be asked to take their meals or share a sleeping-room with the servants, nor are they expected to undertake rough work, such as scrubbing, blacking boots or carrying heavy weights upstairs'. *The Spectator* (16 July 1892) commented that: 'except in the case of a housekeeper, it is quite impossible in an ordinary household to segregate one or two servants from the others ... If ladies are to go into ordinary household service, to be anything else ... but governesses, housekeepers, or companions, they must be willing to place themselves on a level with the rest of the servants in the house.'

The architecture of Victorian houses, with their multiple storeys, made life very difficult for maids. In 1894, when Elizabeth Banks undertook her 'journalistic adventure' posing as a domestic servant in two different households, she was astonished by the difference in terms of layout and conveniences. The first house, situated near Portman Square in London, was 'large and inconvenient' for the number of servants employed. At the second house, 'Everything was much more convenient and comfortable ... Two of the rooms being on the same floor with the bathroom, the filling of the water-pitchers was an easy matter, and I had only to go down one flight of stairs to carry water to Mrs Brownlow's room.' Elizabeth Banks pointed out that buildings like the Portman Square house might be converted by 'the expenditure of a few pounds in putting in lifts from the basement to the first floor, and fitting the bedrooms with hot- and cold-water pipes, which would do away with the necessity of carrying heavy trays and water-cans up and down the stairs.'

Perhaps the suggestion made in the *Lancet*, (quoted in the *Liverpool Mercury*, 6 April 1899), was the most sensible of all. Having noted that chlorotic anaemia was one of the commonest of ailments in domestic servants, the journal commented:

> *An anaemic girl will be sent up long flights of stairs on trivial errands, or a willing maid will be made to do nursing duty till her feet swell, and she is on the point of breaking down. We believe that the alternative employments which draw girls from domestic service would not be so effective if good mistresses determined to ... make their servants feel that they are in a home where their health and their comfort are considered in a kindly and generous spirit.*

No such common sense advice featured in any of the various 'solutions' put forward by employers. They universally failed to address the root of the issue: the personal relationship between mistress and maid, and their attitudes towards one another. Many frustrated employers simply started to use 'dailies' instead of having a live-in servant.

Louise Jermy

Housemaid and Cook

Born in Romsey, Hampshire in 1877, Louise Jermy (née Withers) left school at 11 to help in her stepmother's home-based laundry business. This extremely heavy work, coupled with the physical abuse meted out by her stepmother, took its toll on Louise's health. By the age of 13, she was partially disabled due to tubercular hip disease.

Still needing to earn money, she started a dressmaking apprenticeship but was unable to complete it due to ill-health. In spite of her father's opposition, Louise was determined to leave home and she went into domestic service from 1893 until her marriage in 1911.

This extract is taken from Louise Jermy's autobiography, *The Memories of a Working Woman* (1934), and it is reproduced by kind permission of the British Library. © The British Library Board (Shelfmark 10824.a.19)

One morning after the usual nag, my stepmother suddenly said to me, "I think it time you learnt to do something, suppose you go and scrub out your bedroom for once, instead of me, for a change." Well, I'd always made my own bed … and kept it dusted, certainly I had never done any scrubbing … I could not kneel without support. Although I hardly knew how I should manage I thought I'd try, and so I did the scrubbing lying on my left side. I could not keep getting up and down, so when I moved the pail, I dragged myself after it, and … I finished the job … It was extraordinary how pleased I felt. True my hip was very sore over it but I began to see a way out now, I found I was not so helpless.

She was always saying there was nothing like service for girls and so I said, "Well then, I'll go to service but I won't go about here." Not that I was shamed at being a servant, but I meant to get away where she could not easily interfere with me. She was surprised, [and] told me to go to Duke Street [Registry Office] … I felt it was a way out, and I was glad, for I really had been afraid of what I would do to her if she did not leave me alone …

I got there and gave my name in and was told to take my place in the waiting room. After waiting an hour or two, the clerk asked me if I would live in

Kensington or did I want something nearer home? I said I did not mind so she said, "This lady is not offering much wages, but you know you've got everything to learn and she will train you, so if she will take you, I should advise you to go to her." I saw this lady, who told me that she and her brothers had decided to make a home together, and that they were just moving in. She had got a woman in to scrub and clean the house and help them to get straight. She read Madame's reference [*the dressmaker to whom Louise was apprenticed*] which she had given me when I'd left, and she asked me if Madame would give me a reference for honesty, etc. supposing she wrote for one. I said, "Yes." ...

"Well," said she, "I will write to Madame and supposing everything is satisfactory, could you come on Saturday? I want someone to come at once." This was Thursday. I told her that I had no cotton dresses or anything ready. She said, "Well, never mind, come without ..." I could hardly realise it as I travelled all the way back by bus that I was to make a complete change so soon ...

My stepmother could hardly believe it when I ... told her ... and when father heard about it he was furious ... I spent his sovereign which he threw down, in stuff for cotton dresses, a pair of house shoes and some aprons. My stepmother gave me an old box of her own, and on Saturday she took me to my new place. I did not want her to come with me, but she would, and on the way she gave me two pieces of advice. One was, "Never talk about your master's affairs, they don't concern you or anyone else nor tell anyone anything about the house." The other was, "If at any time anyone should call while your people are out, never let them come in, especially a man, remember you will be all alone there and if they once got in you could not prevent them from ransacking the house. If they are genuine, they will come back again, and if they are not, well you are on the safe side." And so she left me and I won't deny that that first evening, I felt lonely and strange.

I soon settled down in my new home, although at first every bone in my body ached from the unaccustomed work, but I set myself to it. My wages were only £7 a year, which is 11s 8d per month ... my first outlay was in some liniment or oils to rub my hip, for I had set myself to get it well if I could, so I was always nursing it up and coaxing the stiffness out of it ... And as I was always moving about I always took care to go upstairs and down quietly, never rushed at anything, it was truly wonderful the way I improved.

I was always at liberty to go out after the evening dinner, if I wished, and so I nearly always went for a short walk ... I attended the church at the top of the road every Sunday, but I was always alone, but somehow I never cared about it.

I went home for the monthly outing every month, and all who saw me remarked on the change and told me how much better I looked.

I think everybody was surprised that I did not return home, and none more so than my own people, but I was happy where I was, and Miss _____ arranged many little pleasures for me. Once she arranged for me to go to the Earl's Court Exhibition, with some other girls, paying my fare for me, and also giving me two and six to spend. Another time, she and her brother were in some theatricals, given for some charity, at St George's Hall, the piece being "The Magistrate". She was sure I would like to go … and gave me a ticket …

Just about Xmas time, my stepmother began again about money and telling me I ought to ask for more. I stood out for some time, but eventually I did so, and got a rise of one pound. Miss _____ told me she could not afford to pay more. Well, I was content, but my people were not, and finally I was worried into giving notice. The misery I went through that time one would not believe, regret for leaving, fear of new places, dread of being at home for any length of time, nearly made me ill …

So I left, and was at home for Easter, and then got a place as a housemaid. But oh, it was dreadful, it really needed a big, strong woman to do all that had to be done, and the stairs, there were nearly eighty of them; and two of the young ladies rode bicycles and I had to clean them every day. Another thing, I had to share a bedroom with two other girls, and there was only just a space between our beds; a long, low, narrow room, there seemed no air, and certainly no privacy. I could not attend to my hip, as I'd been doing, and by the end of three months I was all to pieces. I took my quarter's wages at the rate of fourteen pounds per year, but what good was it to me? I went home ill, and it was three months before I was fit to go anywhere.

I said to myself … the first good chance that comes of getting right away I'll take it, I'll be free, and make my own way. Aunt Fannie … had been in [a] house as caretaker while these people were away, and as they wanted someone she spoke for me. I went to see this lady, Mrs Muirhead, and was engaged …

Mrs Muirhead gave me a rise the first month I was there and I'll say at once that I loved this lady, I thought her wonderful, and she was too. Mr Muirhead was in some College … and she herself was a mistress of languages, Latin, Greek, French, German, it seems she knew everything, yet she took great interest in me. There were hundreds of books and I was at liberty to read any I liked. One evening she came into the kitchen and found me reading the cookery book, and she sat down and we had a most interesting chat. Another time I had a geography book, and she fetched an orange, and sitting on an easy chair in the kitchen while I sat on the fender, she rapidly drew with her penknife, places all over the world, drew lines for the equator, and told me the reason of different seasons in different places, the reason of light and darkness, and why times differed in places. I daresay she spent an hour with me, and I know I kept that orange as long as ever I could.

On Saturday, sometimes they would cycle into the country, and on those occasions the dinner being very late, she would put on a pinafore over her dress and would come and help me to wash up, helping right to the last, even drying the saucepans and putting them away, after which she would stay for a short chat. Yet she was a perfect lady to her finger-tips and I thought there was nobody on earth so good or clever ...

[*The Muirheads went to Brittany for the summer*] Mr Muirhead had not been home many days when the offer came to go to the Mason College at Birmingham, which afterwards became the Birmingham University. He accepted the post and from that time was called Professor. Mrs Muirhead said to me, "We have decided to go, will you go with us? We should both like it." I said, "Yes," at once ...

So I went away to Birmingham, and in the course of a few years I met many wonderful people ... There was always, every week, a dinner party for the various notable people who came to the College, and on these occasions I both cooked and served the dinner. Afterwards, when all was over, I always went into the drawing-room for a few minutes chat, before going to bed ...

I made many of her things for her, and often saw to her evening gowns, darned and mended linen, and knitted the Professor's socks, and in the year in which he brought out his book, "Political Economy" by J H Muirhead, I did the whole of the house-keeping, served the weekly dinners, when we would draw up the menu together ...

Of course it made a lot for me to do and at times was a great strain ... Towards the close of the winter, I began to be seriously troubled at night with my hip. I would go to bed quite all right, only to wake up in an hour or so in dreadful pain, just as if the joints had slipped out of place. I would have to pull myself out of bed and holding on to anything I could I would have to force myself to walk until it slipped back again. It happened so often that my nerves went to pieces ... and want of sleep meant headache, and that meant bad temper ... I felt I wanted to get away and rest and so at last, I'm sorry to say in a burst of temper, I left ...

I got myself lodgings for a time, and rested, and then took another place, but here the master died when I had only been there two days ... And so I left there, and went to live with some people named Churcher; an old gentleman and his son and daughter [Miss Alice]. I was cook and there was another maid ... I was very happy there. The quiet, regular hours and work, day by day, always suited me and I was better there than I've ever been in my life. My hip got well; I could run like a hare, and, as I never got out of breath, I often ran hard for the sheer joy of it.

[*At the Churchers' house in Birmingham*] the kitchen window looked on the road; but being above the level we could see all that passed. Immediately facing us was a newly-built house with very beautiful gardens ... To the side all else was fields, on which were always cows and horses or other animals turned out to pasture. The outlook for us was so pleasant we never grew tired of it, at any rate I never did, for the truth is, I never liked London. The kitchen itself was large and lofty, and ... in the corner by the range nearest the window stood a large gas stove, which was at that time one of the most up-to-date, and the cooking was mostly all done on it. For several months in the year the range was only lighted once a week, so as to get hot bath water, and to air the linen cupboards ... My scullery was a very large one, with long shelves and lots of saucepans, everything that could be wanted ...

I always had to cook something in the middle of the day and again at night a late dinner, but everything was done by clockwork ... It was Mr Churcher's rule and so we found that as they were always to the minute, we ourselves were always done too. I did a lot of sewing and each of the girls who lived there with me, one of them three years, I taught to cut out clothes and to make many things, also to knit ... I always made my own dresses, blouses, etc. in fact almost everything that I wore, so I could afford to dress very nicely and I did so; but nearly always in black, although I had some very nice blouses of different colours and materials.

[*Louise went home at Easter and met William Brown, the widowed son of her father's neighbour. They started to correspond and he visited her in Birmingham, asking if she would return to London and continue their acquaintance. Having fallen in love, Louise left the Churchers and went back to London. William then wrote to say he had made a mistake and that after his first unhappy marriage, he did not think he would ever marry again.*]

It would have been kinder to have put a knife through me, I should at least have been at rest. As it was, he had struck my life's happiness from me at one blow, and all the best that was in me went with it. My faith and trust in him and in people in general, was gone for ever. I could not get rest anywhere ...

And within three months of going to London, I was cook in a doctor's house in Wimpole Street. Shall I ever forget it? The kitchen was almost entirely underground, and we never saw daylight properly, electric light was on all day, and the beastly beetles sickened me – I've always had a dread of beetles. Life was a nightmare. In my early girlhood I had had training in keeping things to myself, and I did so now … There were five of us girls, and this was the only place I ever took when I had a kitchen maid, for the one experience was quite enough for me. No daylight, no sun, shut in where I could see nothing; I, who had been used to the country, to looking over the fields, and running out to the garden to watch the opening of almost every fresh flower. Can you imagine what it was to me, apart from the misery I was bearing in silence? … I knew nobody, and except on Sunday alternately, once a fortnight, I did not get out long enough to go home … Wherever I went I carried an aching misery that well-nigh crazed me …

I stayed in the place three month, and then I felt I could bear the darkness no longer; I was feeling deadly sick … so I went home and nursed myself a bit. I was at home about three weeks and then took another place, and another after that …

William came back after the second Xmas I had been in London, but the happy-hearted girl he had come to Birmingham to see was gone, and he found a tired, disillusioned, broken-hearted woman in her place, with wrecked nerves, broken health and extremely uncertain temper … there was no happiness in each other, and we parted again before Whitsun.

I felt wretchedly ill, and when I'd been there twelve months I gave up. It was a dreadfully hard place … and I was offered a substantial rise if I would stay, but it was the keeping up appearances, so that no one could guess how wretched I was, that sapped my strength and broke me down at last …

Then one day when I'd gone out to pass the time away I walked into Oxford Street, and on passing a registry office something made me go in … I gave my name and paid the usual fees, was asked if I was ready to go anywhere at once, did I want permanent or temporary service? I didn't care, I said.

"Well," said the clerk, "there has just been a lady here who … wants someone at once, it's in a dreadful muddle, will you go and see her?" I thought it quite an adventure, so I went. When the maid opened the door, I said to her, "Is it all right? I've had a rotten time." She said, "Yes, kid, take it if you can." So I saw the lady, who was house-keeper for her [invalid] sister, Mrs Harvey … The cook, she said, she had found incapably drunk that morning and had packed her off as soon as she became sufficiently sober. Could I come at once, if references were satisfactory? I had then been in London just about two years and one month ...

So I went to Mrs Harvey, and it was the only place I ever got like what I'd been used to in Birmingham. True it was a flat, but the cooking was good, there was abundance of everything. I did not see the lady herself more than three times, and Mr Harvey I never saw at all. He was a Member of Parliament ... and had his separate chambers; but ... he came every day to see his wife who was seldom well enough to leave her room ... I was there during the Xmas [and] although I had been there such a short time, she and Mrs Clark, the sister, gave me a beautiful handkerchief sachet with half-a-dozen lace-trimmed handkerchiefs in it ...

Mrs Harvey made arrangements for us to go to the Duke of York theatre to see "Miss Hook of Holland" a few days after Xmas. We were to go in the car, the ladies' maid, the other maid and myself ... It was a nice evening and I enjoyed it as much as I ever did anything ...

[*At New Year, William returned again.*] When he came in and took me in his arms, I felt that my worry was all over, and for a time I felt that the past was done, and that we would begin again.

[In January] I had to leave the place where I was getting on so comfortably ... The doctors had said that Mrs Harvey must go away ... so ... the flat [was to] be closed ... I got an engagement almost at once, and in another fortnight found myself in Basset Road, in West Kensington [*working for Mr and Mrs Klein.*].

[*William did not like the fact the Kleins were Jewish and complained that he was not allowed to visit Louise. She asked Mrs Klein's permission for him to visit which was granted, but he only came twice. Then William suddenly suggested getting married and moving to Canada, but after receiving advice from Mrs Klein, Louise broke off the relationship for good.*]

[*The Kleins went on holiday for six weeks or so.*] I stayed there very quietly – there were plenty of books. Roberts [the other maid] was older than myself and quiet like myself, and so we had a change and rest; we did the cleaning at our leisure ... I admit that there were times when I ... felt I must have him back, cost what it might, but as time went on I felt it less. There was plenty to do, especially when Mr Leonard came home between terms from Oxford. Then there was a good deal of entertaining, and Mrs Klein planned little pleasures for us sometimes ...

The next summer Mrs Klein took a house in Gloucestershire for the summer holidays ... Mrs Klein kept open house all the time we were there, which was about two months ... There was so much work and cooking, that I was tired out, and glad enough to be settled again in London ...

The extra work and the long hours of almost every day and the busy weekends, when there was sure to be a reception of some kind on the Sunday, was a great strain on me ... yet I was loath to make any change if I could possibly help it, as I gave them satisfaction and that was something; besides I got used to the place and liked it ...

One day I was sick, bringing up rather a large quantity of blood. Of course I went to a doctor, who told me I had got a large ulcer in the stomach ... I began to see plainly that I could not go on like it, and ... that I must have a little room of my own ... where I could rest quietly, and go out to temporary places only, or go out in the season as waitress, or to cook a dinner sometimes. I told myself I would do this as soon as I could get enough money together to start, and a hundred pounds I considered would make it safe to venture ... Thus I planned my life, and so I held on as best I could, saying nothing to nobody.

One morning, [there was] an urgent call from Oxford. Mr Leonard had over-studied and was on the verge of a nervous breakdown ... They got him to Cromer and the rest and quiet pulled him round ... When Mrs Klein came back, she had got [a house for the summer] at Wroxham [in Norfolk] ...

[At Wroxham] ... I was always free to go out as soon as the dinner was served, and so ... John [the gardener] and I just drifted together. The simple goodness of the man appealed to me, and I always felt that here at least was a man whose word never failed ... And then one day he told me he would like to have me for his wife ... And so I gave my promise.

[In February 1911] I married him in the teeth of all opposition [from her father], and for ten years this good man shielded me with a care and kindness I had never known since I left my grandmother, a baby almost, and with a quiet, steady love that never wavered, and when he died, I was left desolate indeed.

Louise and John had two sons together. After John died some ten years later, Louise took on laundry work on a country estate. She died in 1952.

Elizabeth L. Banks

Housemaid and Parlourmaid

Elizabeth Banks was an American journalist who settled in London in around 1893. She undertook a series of 'adventures' in which she posed as a laundry girl, a crossing sweeper, a flower girl, a chaperone, an heiress and a domestic servant. In working as a maid, she hoped to discover why domestic service 'was looked upon with so much contumely'.

Originally published as 'In Cap and Apron' in the *Weekly Sun*, this extract is taken from *Campaigns of Curiosity: Journalistic Adventures of an American Girl in London* (F. Tennyson Neely, 1894). It is not clear how much artistic licence Elizabeth used when describing her time in domestic service but she does provide some interesting details about the duties of staff in households where three or four servants were employed.

After arranging with a titled friend to provide a reference as to her respectability and honesty, Elizabeth placed an advertisement in a national newspaper in the 'Situations Wanted' column. She described herself as a 'refined and educated young woman, obliged to earn her living, and unable to find other employment', who wanted a situation as a housemaid, parlourmaid or house-parlourmaid.

Mrs Allison, residing in a large house in the neighbourhood of Portman Square, wrote to inform me that my reference was satisfactory, and she would give me a place as housemaid. She ended by saying: "I think I shall be able to smooth over many of the rough places for you, and give you a comfortable home."

The parlourmaid [Annie] … led me to the servants' room on the fifth floor. I was immediately struck with the cheerless and comfortless aspect of the place where I was to sleep … Three iron bedsteads stood in a row, and in front of each was a strip of ragged carpet …

In the kitchen I found Annie standing before the fire grilling mutton chops. She explained that a new cook would be there the following Monday and that she was to prepare the meals until then. "Been out to service before?" [she asked].

"No; this is my first place."

"You'll find it's not so easy as it looks," she remarked, with a very superior and knowing air. "We're on board wages till the cook comes," she continued. "There's your allowance on the shelf." ...

Later in the evening we made the round of the rooms. Annie gave me explicit instructions as to how to tidy them up, turn down the beds and make the washstands ready for use. When this work was done, I was more tired than I had ever been in my life. What with emptying out the washbowls and refilling the pitchers, I had gone up and down two flights of stairs eight times, carrying heavy water-cans and pails.

[*Mrs Allison called Elizabeth to the study and gave her a list of the work she was to do the next day.*]

I was to rise at six in the morning, and my first duty was to shake and brush Mr Allison's trousers, which I would find hanging on the doorknob outside his room ... the second duty ... was to brush Mrs Allison's dress and carry all the boots to the kitchen for Annie to polish ... Afterwards I would sweep and dust four flights of stairs and five halls, clean up and dust the study and drawing-rooms, and carry a can of hot water to each person, knocking on the door to wake him or her up.

[*These duties were all to be completed before breakfast.*]

[Mrs Allison continued:] "After you have breakfasted, Lizzie, you must help Annie with the dishes, then make the beds, clean up the washstands, fill the water-jugs, sweep and dust the bedrooms, attend to the candlesticks, and put everything in perfect order in the sitting-rooms. You will get this done by eleven o'clock. From eleven till three, you will turn out one or two of the rooms and eat your dinner in the meantime. At four o'clock I want you to be dressed with clean cap and apron. Then you will get the servants' afternoon tea and clear it away, and you can fill up the time until supper with needlework." After supper I was to make the round of the rooms again and sew until a quarter-past-ten. Then I might go to bed ...

After hearing the "list", I bowed politely to Mrs Allison, said, "Very well, ma'am," and joined Annie in the kitchen. She greeted me with a fiendish grin, and said, "Did she say anything about the scrubbing?"

"Scrubbing! Must I scrub?" I almost shrieked.

"You'll think so, when you get at it! Why, you have to scrub a bedroom all over every day, and sometimes two! You see, you must turn out a room each day, and there's no carpet on the bedrooms; only a narrow rug before the bed. On turning out day, you must shake the rug and scrub up the floor and the paint. It do make your hands and arms ache, I tell you. It's too bad you took such a hard place for your first time in service!"

[The next morning] the trousers and the dress were duly brushed, the stairs and halls swept and dusted, and each person supplied with a hot-water can. Then I went into the study, which was a large room. There were dozens of ornaments on the desk and mantel, which it seemed an endless task to dust and rearrange. My head ached for the want of food, yet I knew that I had not only the study to finish, but two large drawing-rooms to attend to. I noticed that the drawing-rooms and the study were the only really cheerful rooms in the house. All the comforts and pictures and ornaments were crowded together in these rooms, and to do them up properly was no easy piece of work ... At 8.30 I finished them, however, and went to the kitchen.

Annie informed me that ... if I wanted anything for breakfast besides tea and bread, I must go and buy it ... Remembering that my own home was only a short distance from the place where I was "in service", I ran around there and filled my basket with provisions ... Annie's face beamed when she saw the wonderful purchases ... That morning we breakfasted off mutton chops and tomato sauce, while the family up-stairs were content to start the day with one egg each and a slice of toast.

That first day "in service" lingers in my memory as a sort of nightmare. The whole house seemed arranged in such a way as to make the work as hard as possible. The bath-room was on the top floor, and, as all the water must be carried from there to the bedrooms below, it was no small matter to fill in the water-pitchers. Then, in washing, every member of the family seemed to have taken particular pains to spill as much water about as possible, and everything had to be removed from the wash-stands before they could be put in order ... Eleven o'clock came, and I had not finished the bedroom work. There were all the candlesticks to scrape off ...

When I had spent two days in Mrs Allison's service, I began to wonder what the "rough places" would have been like had she not attempted to smooth them over. She certainly could not have accused me of being a slow worker, and I did not "dilly-dally" over my duties, yet on Friday and Saturday I found it impossible to make time for "turning out" the rooms, however much I hurried. I no sooner finished tidying up the bedrooms than the washbowls were again filled to overflowing with soapy water and needed further attention. When I had brushed one dress and hung it in the wardrobe, another flannel gown or coat would be hung out on the banisters ... these small things call a servant away from her more important work and put her behind for the whole day ...

I soon became accustomed to my work, and was really surprised at the readiness with which I put into practice all I learned from my little book on "Servants' Duties". Besides the daily sweeping, I was obliged to rub [the felted stairs] frequently with a damp cloth in order to remove the accumulated dust and lint. The halls and passages were of stone, with rugs scattered about, which proved to be perfect traps for dust and dirt ... In the halls, on the stairs, and in every room of the house, from the kitchen to the fifth floor, candle-grease was plentifully sprinkled, and my brown paper and hot flat-iron were in constant demand ...

Sunday morning we were allowed a half-hour's extra sleep; but, to my astonishment, Annie informed me that the same round of work must be done as on weekdays. The stairs and passages, bedrooms, sitting-rooms and drawing-rooms were to be swept and dusted, and I was busy until twelve o'clock as on former days ...

At two o'clock, as a meal for seven persons had to be cooked, Mrs Allison asked me to wait at table while Annie stayed in the kitchen ... I had received a letter ... telling me to call on Mrs Brownlow, in Kensington, at six o'clock Sunday, as she thought she could employ me as parlourmaid. At five I asked permission to go out, which was granted. [I] made arrangements to enter [Mrs Brownlow's] service as parlourmaid the following Thursday evening, though how I should get rid of my current place I had not then decided.

I returned at seven, and found Annie busily engaged in answering the door. It was Mrs Allison's day at home. I helped to prepare the tea and cakes, later we served supper to the family and at nine had our own bread and cheese. So this was a Sunday in service. I had two hours' rest; Annie had none! ...

Monday evening the new cook made her appearance, and our board wages ceased ... For breakfast, Tuesday, bread and butter and coffee were placed on the table.

"Is there no meat or potatoes?" I questioned Annie.

"No, the missus never allows us anything in the morning but bread and coffee."

I was already tired with my morning's work, and, having been told I must "turn out" two rooms that day, I knew that, without a proper breakfast, I should not be able to get through. I would speak to Mrs Allison about it.

"Better not," said Annie; "the last cook fried some fish for breakfast one morning, and she got notice."

"Annie," I said, "I'm afraid this place is going to be too hard for me. I don't think I'll stop after my week is up."

"But you can't leave without giving notice. If you do, she'll make you pay her a whole month's wages; and, if she makes you go without giving notice, she must pay you a month's wages," explained my co-worker.

"But suppose I do something she doesn't like and she discharges me?"

"Why, then, you'd have to go; but she wouldn't give you a character."

I went to Mrs Allison's room and knocked at the door.

"Mrs Allison, do you not allow the servants anything for breakfast but bread and coffee? I thought there must be some mistake," I said, as she opened the door.

"No, it is not a mistake," was her reply.

"But I must have a good breakfast or I simply cannot do the work, so I will go out and buy some meat myself."

"Very well, do so," she answered as she shut the door.

An hour later, I was making her bed, when she entered the room.

"Lizzie, I have been thinking it over, and I have decided that you and I won't pull," was her announcement.

"No, I don't think we will, Ma'am," I replied.

"Then, if you will wait until I get suited," she continued, "you may go."

I told her I was sorry I could not accommodate her, but that I preferred to leave Thursday and she went off in high dudgeon, saying that any common servant would show her mistress the courtesy to remain until she was suited. Thus it came to pass that I was discharged from my first place without a character because I, like Oliver Twist, had the audacity to "ask for more" ...

Annie's duties [as a parlourmaid] were to rise at six o'clock, attend to the lamps, sweep and dust the large music-room, carry some boiling water to Mrs Allison, lay the table, wait at all the meals, clear away and brush up afterwards, answer the door, and assist with the needlework. Her duties seemed neither so numerous nor so complex as my own, but ... from half-past nine in the morning until eleven at night the bell rang on an average of every ten minutes ...

On Wednesday afternoon, the decree came forth that I should take up all the rugs in the drawing-room and scrub the floor ... I dared not confide my ignorance to anyone, for when I engaged with Mrs Allison, I assured her that I had never been a servant, but had learned how to work at home ...

In scrubbing that drawing-room I kept two ideas in mind: first, to ward off housemaid's knee; second, to keep myself and costume out of the wet. So pinning up my frock, I took the brush and assumed a squatting position, hopping about from place to place. I scrubbed a square yard at a time, then rinsed in clean water and dried it ... I had nearly finished, when, glancing toward the folding-doors, I saw Mrs Allison looking at me, her large black eyes burning with anger ...

"Well, a pretty servant you make, I must say! Any girl with half a grain of sense would know how to scrub. You haven't even got general intelligence!" was the announcement that burst from her ... I had nothing to say in my own defence; but a sense of the ridiculous overcame my prudence, and I smiled blandly in Mrs Allison's face. She uttered a contemptuous, impatient "Oh!" and left me ...

Mrs Allison did not speak to me again after the scrubbing episode. [On Thursday] at six o'clock I informed her that I was ready to go, she silently handed me six shillings, which was really liberal, for she only owed me five shillings and fourpence halfpenny. I thanked her and said good-bye, but she did not answer ...

Mrs Brownlow's residence was a pretty little house in Kensington ... I was admitted by the housemaid [Alice] ...

In a corner [of the dining-room] Alice called my attention to a lift, connecting the kitchen and dining-room. She explained that, before laying the table, I was to put all the china on the lift and draw it up, and that the cook would send up the meats and vegetables just as the family sat down.

"You'll have to toe the mark if you keep this place," said she confidentially. "Missus sent the last parlourmaid away because she didn't make the glasses shine and broke so many dishes. Just before she left she broke a big punch-bowl and a lot of cups, and never told. Missus found it out a few hours before she went, and took out a part of her wages for it. It was a shame, wasn't it?"

"Why, no, I don't think so. What right had she to break the dishes and not say anything about it? And, besides, if it was her fault, she ought to pay for them," I answered, for the moment putting myself in Mrs Brownlow's place and feeling that I should have done the same thing under similar circumstances.

A very unpleasant look gathered on Alice's face as I said it.

"Oh! so you take the part of the missus against the servants, do you? I don't."

From that time I knew I had an enemy.

[I had my own room which] Mrs Brownlow had just fitted up for me ... Under the mantel there was a small gas-grate. Alice told me there were not coal-fires in the house, and that even the cooking was done by gas ...

At eight o'clock we had our own dinner, which consisted of a joint, potatoes, brussels sprouts, and a boiled pudding. There were four of us – Sarah the cook, Janette the French maid, Alice and myself ... I learned that usually the family and the servants ate the same food … After dinner Alice went up-stairs to tidy the rooms, and I remained in the kitchen until about half-past nine.

When Mrs Brownlow returned, I was asked to go to her room … She explained that in employing me she was making an experiment, and, if she found it a successful one, she would make an entire change in her staff of servants, and engage girls of education to take the places of the cook and housemaid.

Before leaving I was given the following list of the parlourmaid's duties:

"Rise at seven o'clock, and be ready for the servants' breakfast at 7.15. Afterwards sweep and dust the front hall and drawing-room, lay the table for the nine o'clock breakfast, wait at table and clear away, attend to the glass and silver, light gas-fires in drawing- and dining-rooms, sweep and dust the dining-room, clean the lamps, lay the table for one o'clock luncheon, clear away, prepare for dinner and wait at table. After each meal shake the crumb-cloth, and answer the door during the day. Always to be dressed in time for luncheon."

Besides this daily round, a part of each day in the week was to be given to some special work, such as turning out the drawing-room, dining-room, cleaning silver &c. On Saturday I was to assist the housemaid in airing and repairing the table and bed linen, the needlework of the family being done by the ladies' maid. I was to have an afternoon off each week, and be allowed to go to morning or evening service on Sunday, if I desired. On Sunday it was arranged that each servant should have half the day to herself, and the cook had every Sunday afternoon off, a mid-day dinner being served, and either Alice or I preparing and clearing away the eight o'clock supper.

Mrs Brownlow's list did not terrify me as Mrs Allison's had done for the amount of work required was not unreasonable, and there was no starting with the day's work without breakfast. Mrs Brownlow told me she had experienced considerable trouble in regard to the cleaning of knives, blacking of boots, and scrubbing the front step, each servant declaring it was the other's place to do these things, until finally she had procured the services of a member of the Houseboy's Brigade, who came every morning to do this work, while once a week a larger boy from the same place washed all the windows in the house …

At 7.15 the next morning we sat down to the kitchen breakfast, which consisted of fried bacon, potatoes, toast and coffee … Mrs Brownlow was one of the most considerate women I had ever met, and tried in every way to make her servants comfortable; but neither the cook nor Alice showed any appreciation of her kindness. Both of them were continually on the defensive, and seemed to believe that mistress and servant must necessarily look upon each other as enemies … I began to wonder if, after all, good treatment was appreciated by many of the girls who went out to service, and I decided that it did not always follow that a kind mistress made a good servant ...

"Why do you not wipe the hot-water cans before you set them in the hall?" I said one morning to Alice, who had been distributing the water at the different bedroom doors.

"Because it's too much trouble," she answered, with a toss of her head.

"But you will ruin the carpet," I insisted.

"Well, it's not your carpet, so you will please mind your own business," she retorted.

Now, what could be done with a girl so perfectly devoid of honour? I asked her how she expected to keep a situation, and how she could get a character, if she did not try to please her mistress.

"Well, I'd make a time if she wouldn't give me a character," was her answer, as she went to the next floor dripping water over the stairs.

And she did "make a time"; for the very next day Mrs Brownlow, losing all patience with her because she would not turn the mattresses or even take the quilts entirely off before making the beds, said, "Alice, I cannot put up with your careless habits any longer, and I wish you would look for a new situation. I give you notice to-day."

Alice replied, "I'll go to-day if you'll give me a month's wages and let me have a character."

"It will be impossible for me to give you a character, unless it is a very bad one," answered her mistress.

And then the "time" commenced. Alice threatened her with all the dreadful consequences imaginable; said she knew certain things she would tell all over London, and accused Mrs Brownlow of taking the bread out of her mouth. She did not become quiet until Mr James Brownlow came in and gave her what he described as a "dressing down", when she slunk away to the kitchen ...

However, she did not leave that day, probably deciding that it would be better to remain her month out, with the hope that she might, after all, obtain the "character" to help her secure another situation. On Sunday she took her half-day off, going out immediately after breakfast, and I did the bedroom work that morning ...

With the assistance of Janette, I was through all the work by eleven o'clock, and was able to rest until it was time to lay the table for the two o'clock dinner. In the afternoon I remained in my room [and wrote] a long letter to the Editor of the *Weekly Sun*. I requested him to look up for me a superior young woman, thoroughly domesticated, who would be willing to take a situation as parlourmaid in Mrs Brownlow's house when I left ... Then I made arrangements to have a telegram sent me on Wednesday requesting my presence in the City that afternoon on important business, which would appear to give me a plausible excuse for resigning my situation.

That night I slept the sleep of the just, and awoke Monday morning feeling fortified against all the attacks of Alice, my enemy ... I became quite an expert in laying and waiting on the table, and I grew proud of my skill in making it look beautiful with bright china and silver ...

[*Elizabeth's pre-arranged telegram arrived and she resigned her situation. She arranged for Lucy Atkins, a 'refined and quiet' physician's daughter and acquaintance of one of the staff at the Weekly Sun, to replace her as parlourmaid at Mrs Brownlow's.*]

I have come to the conclusion that there are as many ill-treated mistresses as servants in London. I found Mrs Allison to be an unjust and unreasonable mistress, demanding more work of her servants than she had any right to expect. With such a large and inconvenient house as hers, she needs to keep at least two strong, healthy housemaids to do the work properly ... Annie, who was a girl accustomed to hard work from her childhood, had been obliged to exchange her place as housemaid for what she thought might be the lighter duties of parlourmaid, and her predecessor had worked herself into the hospital.

Mrs Brownlow, on the other hand, was kind and considerate with her servants. She gave them too much liberty, and thought more of their comfort than of her own well-being. Her house had been fitted up with a view of making the work light and easy of accomplishment, and three servants should have done all the work and had plenty of leisure for rest and recreation. Alice and the cook were most ungrateful and neglectful, and did not in any way endeavour to please ...

Taking service as it is at present, I think that the position of a domestic servant with a reasonable mistress and in a conveniently-arranged house is far superior to that of the sewing-girl, the factory-girl, or the struggling stenographer and book-keeper in the City. There are hundreds of places like Mrs Brownlow's, where employment can be found for girls who are not receiving the much-discussed "living wage" and for those girls, surely, domestic work is preferable to their present employment.

From the servant-owning class herself, Elizabeth Banks had no particular desire to bring about reform for servants. In her autobiography, she admitted that her real reason for going into service had been 'that I might get a start in English journalism and thus put myself in a fair way of earning my own living in London'. She had a long career in journalism and died in London in 1938.

Amy Grace Rose

Nursemaid, Housemaid and Cook

Amy Grace Rose (née Andrews) was born in 1877 in Great Shelford, Cambridgeshire. Often known as Grace, she was the youngest of eleven children. Her father was a farm labourer earning just ten shillings a week, so the family struggled to make ends meet. Her mother did fine needlework for upper-class customers like the Duchess of Leeds.

The family's financial situation worsened when Grace's father had an accident and was unable to work, and her mother could no longer get sufficient needlework to support them. She took in two babies to nurse, Mary and Archie; Grace took charge of Archie and did all the housework. She went into domestic service from the age of 22 until her marriage in 1904.

The following extract about her time in domestic service has been taken from Grace's unpublished reminiscences, which she wrote in 1949 when she was about 72. It has been reproduced with the kind permission of Cambridgeshire Archives, where the surviving document is held (P137/28/3). The original spellings have been retained throughout.

Archie started school so I had a little more leisure or time on my hands and I began to think it was time I was earning my own living. But Mother said why couldn't I be satisfied as I was and I should only get ill but I said I'll not have to work much harder than I do now ... My Father never seemed to get much better and he used to stay in bed a lot. He told me to go if I wished ... So I wrote to [Miss Bullock], a Lady I knew who lived in Cambridge who used to be my Sunday school teacher ... [I] told her I wanted to go away from home and she wrote almost at once to say yes, she did know of someone who wanted a girl, a Nurse maid for her children but it was at Lowestoft – did I mind going so far away from home. I thought the farthest the better ... and she sent me the Lady's address so I wrote to Lowestoft ...

I never got an answer to my letter as the Lady's Husband came to see me ... He looked at me very kindly and he said he was Mr Stubbs and as he was in

Cambridge that day, his Wife asked him if he would come over and see me. He said they had had a very nice letter from my friend who had spoke very well of me and had said she was sure I was to be trusted ... He smiled again and said he was sure I would be alright, and spoke very nicely to my Mother, and asked her about me ... course she was on her best behaviour and spoke civil and nice to him and told him I was not too strong and never had been. All he said to her was the Sea air might be good for me and it was too, for I'd never been so well in my life as I was there. When he got up to go he said Mrs Stubbs would send my train fare and all particulars later ... Two or three days after, the letter came as promised and all instructions about the journey and being met at Lowestoft.

I was met by a Nurse in Uniform. She said her name was Patterson but she was usually called Nurse Patty and she had been looking after Mrs Stubbs who had got a New Baby which made three. But I'd have nothing to do for the New Baby as the Misstress would look after it herself ... [there was] the little girl aged four whose name was Kathleen but was always called Diddy and Alan the Boy who they called Stick. The New Baby was to be called Dorothy but in time was called Tinker. Mrs Stubbs was in bed when we got to Gordon Road and the house was number 22, just my own age ... the Lady took hold of my hand and asked if I liked Babies. I said yes, I loved them and I told her about Archie and how I had to do everything for him. Then she gave me a kind smile and said I am sure I can trust you with my Babies and I felt I could have worshipped her for saying that and how kind she was ... I seemed never to have had such kindness in my life before ... I felt I could not do enough for them and the children soon got to know and love me, and I felt myself full of happiness and love for them for all.

I stayed with them a good while and should not have left, but had a letter from my mother saying she was not well and I was to leave as soon as I could as she had nobody to look after her. Oh, I was sorry for I was very happy and feeling better than I had ever done in all my life ... So I went home and left all my happiness behind me ... I went in at the door and there sat my mother in her chair by the Table reading and looking as well as usual ... I said I thought you were ill. She said I have been queer a bit but I'm better now. I said whatever did you send for me to come home for if you are better, and could say no more for I was crying ... [Father] was pleased to see me and then suddenly I was so pleased I had come home if only to see Father.

Mother said Mrs Rudge up at Granhams House at Shelford wants a girl, you'd better go and see about the place in the morning, and I thought so that's what you sent for me home for. But I never said anything but went to see her in the morning … I got the job alright and the Lady was so pleased to see me that I thought you would have taken anybody as long as they could work …

I found the work at the Granhams House very hard. I had only been doing my Night and Day Nurseries at Lowestoft and seen after the children all the rest of the day. Even my meals had been brought up to me with the Children's. So I found the work was harder than I had bargained for. The cook was nice, but I had to get to Granhams at seven in the morning, do the Kitchen range and light the fire, boil the Kettle and take cook a pot of Tea and some Biscuits upstairs. Then I had to come down and lay the Kitchen table ready for Breakfast. There was cook, a House parlour maid, two Laundry women and myself. Five of us in the Kitchen to do for. Then I had to sweep and scrub the front steps, sweep and dust the Hall before I had Breakfast.

By the time I was ready to go to the Kitchen the others were nearly finished theirs. After Breakfast, I had to clear the table, help the parlour maid in the pantry, take the Nursery Breakfast up – there were three children and a Nursery Governess who was very nice to me and showed me just how she liked the table fixed. And the children were darlings, with lovely blue eyes, and fair curly hair, and such sweet faces. I could have loved them very much. When the Nursery Breakfast was finished I had all the things to fetch down again, to wash up.

After that I had to help the House parlour maid with the Beds and bedrooms, help her turn one room thoroughly out, and dust. After that, I had to get all the vegetables ready pared and washed for cook's Lunch time, wash all her cookery things up, and turn out the Kitchen, and wash it all over. Also clean all the Knives, fill Scuttles for Nursery, Study, Dining room, Drawing room, and Breakfast room. Oh and the scuttles were heavy when they were filled. I thought I'd never be able to do it all in the time. After I had filled all the scuttles, I had to help the parlour maid lay the dining room table for Lunch, then go back to the Kitchen and do what I could to help Cook with the dishing up. Also in between lay the Kitchen table for ours.

Oh dear, I began to think I'd never get through, for my legs were tired and my head began to ache. And after Lunch, which was our Dinner, there was all the heaps and heaps of washing up to be done, Nursery things as well. Cook went up to lay on her bed, and left me all alone in the Kitchen, and I could have cryed. I believe I did too. After I had finished it was time to get the Kitchen Tea, and I thought, I wish I were home. For after Tea there was all the cooking to do over again for dinner at Seven. And after Dinner all the washing up to be done. So it was nearly nine o'clock before I could get my hat and coat and leave it all. The Cook called out, don't be late in the morning. I said to myself, let me get home first. Oh I was tired, and I had all that long way to walk home. I was so tired that I went straight up to bed …

The next morning seemed to come very quickly … I was in good time, but still felt very tired, and wondered how I should get through the day. When I reached the Granhams it looked all wrapped in slumber. I found the Key and unlocked the door. The Supper table was cleared, but the things were waiting in the Scullery to be washed up. I did the Stove and lit the fire as yesterday, used a few more sticks so got the Kettle boiling as quickly as I could, took Cook's cup of Tea up, came down and laid the Kitchen table for Breakfast, then did my steps, and the Hall, and dusted down the Stairs, polished the floor cloth in the Hall. [I] put too much polish on, for Mrs Rudge's Brother, who made his home at the Granhams, came running down to the Breakfast room, stepped on the Mat at the bottom of the stairs, and went sliding nearly the whole length of the Hall, before he sat down with a bump, which of course brought all the rest out of the room. How they laughed. I stood there trembling, wondering if I should be sent home, and what Mother would say if I did. When the Gentleman at last had done laughing, he came to me and gave me a shilling, and said, Thank you for a good appetite for Breakfast. All Mrs Rudge said was I shouldn't polish it tomorrow if I was you. I never heard any more about it and the day passed as the day before, just keeping on, and I was so tired, more tired than yesterday and could hardly walk home.

The next morning I woke up with a dreadful Head and my legs were aching fit to drop off. I thought, Oh dear, I don't believe I shall do it today. I was so tired and done up that I had to sit down before I lit the fire but only just tidied the stove, could not clean it. And when I took Cook's tea up, she sat up in bed, and she said whatever's the matter with you. I said I feel very tired, that's all, and started to cry. She said don't cry, I'll get up, which she did. When she came down stairs, she made me drink a cup of Tea, and said you'll be all right presently, but I wasn't. I just sat there and cried and cried. Cook said when the Misstress gets down, I will go and tell her, and perhaps she will let you go home. When Cook knew the Misstress had come down, she went and told her I was not very well. The Misstress came out into the Kitchen, and stood a minute and then said she was sure I'd feel better when I had had some Breakfast. I tried to eat some, and felt a bit better, but if anyone spoke to me, I would start crying again.

Cook did all she could, and saved me as much work as was possible, and I got through the day somehow. The Cook let me go home as soon as I had helped her Dish up the Dinner, and said the washing up could be left for the morning as she would put the plates in the sink and turn the tap on for a little … When I started to walk home, I could hardly put one foot in front of the other. It was late when I got home, and Mother wanted to know where I had been stopping …

When morning came I could not get out of bed. Mother grumbled and said what's the matter? Father in the next room heard, and called out let the girl lay, do. And Mother found that I did have to lay still, for I could not move, only just lift my hand to take the cup of Tea she brought me, but could not drink it. So she let me be, and said I'd better stay at home, and tomorrow I would be better. But tomorrow came, and I still could not go to work.

Mrs Rudge came to see me, and said to Mother you'd better let the Doctor see her. Mother didn't like that much but Mrs Rudge said tell him to send the bill to me. So Mother sent for the Doctor who was a Doctor Magoris, and lived at Shelford … Well, he came up stairs after Mother, and he stood and looked at me, then he turned to Mother, and said what's the girl been doing to get in this state? Mother told him I had only been to the Granhams three or four days. When Mother stopped talking, he took my hand, and said you're not to go back, do you hear me. I said yes, Sir. Mother said she'll lose her Job. The Doctor turned to her and said is the Job worth more to you than your child? …

That ended the Granhams for me. But I think even now after all these years of the terrible days I spent there. Of course I had always done the work of Mother's house, but that was nothing to be compared with the Granhams and I had never had to work so hard for other people …

When I felt well enough to go to work again, our Vicar at Stapleford wanted someone to look after his two children, Irene aged ten and Sidney the Boy seven … I had to bath them and look after them generally, take them to School in the mornings … The Children never went to school in the afternoons so after I had met them at twelve o'clock and got home and had had our dinner, Sidney would have his rest then from three to half past four we could do as we liked after Tea … Then we could play on the lawn or go for a little walk until it was six o'clock when I would see to their Bath and help them to bed … Then I would sometimes go down and help the other maid with the dining room dinner, lay the table and do what I could. I did not have to do [it] but I liked helping and Edith the maid was good to me. As there was only one room to spare and it was not big enough for two beds, so Edith used to go home to sleep … Edith and I got on well together and used to help each other.

Then the Children got Flue and whooping cough and I was running about all day long with bowls and towels and things, it was a time. The Misstress got the Flue too and was very ill and the Children and I weren't allowed in her room.

One Evening after the children were in bed I lay down on the outside of Irene's bed and was reading to them as I often did ... The next morning I woke up with a terrible Headache and my legs were all wobbley, and cold shivers running down my back ... I was in bed two weeks and when I tried to get up my legs were almost useless ... The Vicar came and told me that they could not wait any longer for me as Mrs Wyman was still very ill ... so the vicarage job came to an end. I seemed to be home quite a long time ... I went to see Edith one evening after she had got home for the night ... She told me that the House maid at the Children's School had asked her if she knew of any one who would be able to cook many plain dinners.

So I went the next morning without saying anything to my mother and I was lucky enough to get the job. Oh, I was pleased for I was going to sleep there too ... There was not very much to do really. The Kitchen Fire to get in the morning first thing for Miss Hedleys' cups of tea, for the three young ladies. Their Father didn't like to be wakened up so early so he waited for Breakfast. Then there was their Hot water to take up. Then I swept and dusted the School room. The Housemaid had to do the dining room. Then I used to get on with cooking the Porridge and Bacon or Sausages, whatever there was. The housemaid had to lay the dining room table.

Then after Breakfast my busiest time was over. There was just a few vegetables to get ready, and perhaps a small Roast, and Yorkshire pudding. Sometimes they had just a plain suet pudding with jam, now and then a Spotted Dog, which was Suet pudding with currants in, sometimes Toad in the Hole. But there was nothing very special. Then there was my Kitchen to keep clean, and my own bedroom. So I was not hard worked. After dinner was cleared and I had washed up my cookery things I was finished until Supper as the Housemaid had to get the Dining room Tea, and wash the things up, so I had not to do that. Sometimes I would bake the Ladies a Potato for Supper, for which they would be very pleased. So I really had an easy job.

Some times when the Housemaid was busy upstairs, I would find a book, and sit by the fire, and forget everything else. When I used to think and look at the clock, I'd think of my dinner, and my Fire would be nearly out, and I'd say to myself, I'll have to give them a boiled pudding today, and I'd get away with it alright. Sometimes if I had a nice Fire, and the oven was hot I'd make some Buns for Tea, and sometimes they would burn, but the housemaid used to say, That don't matter, make some more, and I'll take the burnt ones home to my Brother. He'll eat them. I used to like the days when Miss Hedley would say,

Amy, we'll have a Spotted Dog for dinner today, because I knew it would not be any bother.

The three sisters always called me Amy which was my first name because … the Middle one was Grace which I was always called by at home as my name was Amy Grace. The eldest Miss Hedley was Ethel. Then came Grace, then the younger one Winifred. Miss Hedley's Father did not get up to Breakfast, and I remember one morning taking Breakfast up stairs, which was Sausages, and a slice of Fried Bread. And his tea cup held rather a lot, so the tray was a bit heavy, and I just managed to get into His room, when the Sausages went rolling off, and right under the bed. I said, Oh, I am sorry, and I had to grope all under the bed for them. But he just said, that's alright. They won't have lost anything, but I was rather frightened all the same.

[*While working for the Hedleys, Grace met Billy Rose, her future husband, who was the gardener at the house next door.*]

I was at the school a little longer then my Father died. The last time I saw him in bed. He looked so thin and ill and could hardly speak to me but his eyes seemed to smile at me and I kissed him and went back to the school. When I told Miss Hedley she was sorry, and told me not to worry, he would be better off. And then she told me I could go to bed. She herself would get Supper. And in the morning quite soon after Breakfast, a Neighbour of my mother's came to tell me my Father was dead. My poor dear Father. How he suffered and never made a murmur. When it came to Easter Monday, Miss Hedley came into the Kitchen and said … as soon as you have finished you can go … I said I'd rather stay here. She said, we don't like to leave you all alone, and we three are all going out. She said, go down to your sister, I should.

That same day, Billy Rose proposed to Grace and they were married on the August Bank Holiday in 1904. They had one daughter. During the First World War, Billy became crippled with arthritis and Grace took work as a postwoman, did some charring, and later worked in the Chivers factory. She died in 1961.

John Robinson

Butler

In 1892, a series of articles were published in the national press about domestic servants, including pieces by Lady Violet Greville in the *National Review* (February) and Lady Aberdeen in *The Nineteenth Century: a Monthly Review* (March). John Robinson, a butler who had been in domestic service for some 14 years, wrote an article in response to the upper-class employer's point of view for the June issue of *The Nineteenth Century: a Monthly Review* entitled 'A Butler's View of Men-Service'.

The following extract comes from that article, which shows John Robinson to have been a highly intelligent, literate and well-informed man. He provides a valuable insight into men-servants' daily lives and their shortcomings, but also the ways in which they were routinely treated by their employers. Nothing else is known about John Robinson, other than the fact he had served in five different houses.

In the March number of this *Review* Lady Aberdeen records an attempt to do something towards raising the moral and intellectual standard of servant life. For her efforts in this direction Lady Aberdeen deserves the sincerest thanks of all intelligent servants. It appears to me, however, that her ladyship has not, in her experiment struck at the root of the upas-tree. She seeks to apply the remedy before she has ascertained the nature and extent of the wound. The real state of affairs is much more forcibly implied in Lady Violet Greville's episodes of servant life than expressed in Lady Aberdeen's more explicit statement. These episodes, which are by no means caricatures, reveal an amazing amount of ignorance and meanness on the part of the domestic servant. This reputation for meanness and general depravity is abundantly supported from other sources. Plaints are continually being made in the daily papers about the difficulty of getting good servants. The registry offices tell how few names there are without some blemish; and employers are fain to accept the inevitable and be content with a very humble mediocrity of character and attainments in their servants. Finally, the contempt with which the servant is regarded by his employer and by the world at large affords a fairly adequate criterion of his real worth.

It has seemed to me that this inferiority of the modern servant is not, as Lady Aberdeen suggests, due merely to the deterrent conditions which tend to eliminate the better class of men and women, but that certain enervating conditions exist which have a debasing effect on those who actually choose service as a calling. I also believe the latter set of conditions to be much more operative than the former ...

I will begin by accepting the general verdict, and at once admitting that the average man-servant is a very poor creature indeed. Aim he has none beyond that of gaining a sordid livelihood. His daily life is a mean and shallow affair. *Carpe diem* is his motto. In his spare time he will play for hours at a childish game of push-penny. 'Ha'penny nap' ranks with him as an accomplishment, whist means too much mental effort. His wages gravitate to a convenient 'pub' in the shape of drinks and bets on the current big race. He rarely makes any individual effort at self-improvement, consequently he never combines for that end. His ambition never soars beyond the proprietorship of an inn or lodging-house.

Yet this phenomenon finds its place about the vanguard of nineteenth-century civilisation! How infinitely superior was the manly and self-respecting lacquey or major-domo of one hundred years ago to the servile and obsequious servant of modern days! This wretched creature may be seen touching his hat or forelock with every word he utters, conscious of his inferiority to a master morally low. Spectacles like this (and they are frequent) mark a degree of degeneracy alike in master and man; for the love of such homage, from such a source, is certainly incompatible with that magnanimity which in theory at least is one of the prime characteristics of a gentleman.

The scene just described is, moreover, typical of the relationship which subsists between the servant, as a class, and society, in the fashionable sense of the word. The employer has hitherto been accustomed to look on the servant and his peccadilloes as something quite outside of himself. He will be surprised to hear that there is an organic connection between the life the servant leads and that led by himself. To one behind the scenes the terms of this relationship are not difficult to make out. Thus when a man enters service he sacrifices all freedom. Any preconceived notions he may have of living his life in a particular way must be thrown to the winds. He becomes the creature of his surroundings, which are determined by the people with whom he lives.

Accordingly, what a splendid training in gluttony and peculation is usually afforded the young servant when first he enters service! Probably he is heavily handicapped from the first, since he not seldom enters service on the same principle as that on which his employer's boys enter the Church, namely, as being fit for nothing better; consequently he starts with some moral or intellectual shortcoming. Thus inadequately equipped he passes at once from comparative privation to the midst of luxury. If there be, as often is the case, any morbid cravings begotten of the penury of his early life, here is his opportunity. Without any restraint other than that which an embryo conscience affords, he finds himself amongst dainties that would tickle the fancy of a sybarite. Questions as to *meum* and *tuum*, qualms as to the manliness of such indulgence are set aside as squeamish fancies, and the youth is soon well on the way towards making a confirmed thief and sensualist ... [this] describes ... what personal observation leads me to believe takes place in the case of a large percentage of young servants. There is a great lack of efficient supervision. Those in charge are often too indolent, frequently they are gourmands themselves, and so encourage rather than repress this guilty indulgence.

There is another circumstance which greatly tends to encourage enervating practices of this kind. It is commonly supposed that at their legitimate table servants live better than those on a similar plane of well-being out of service. This is in a sense true, but in the case of most households more false than true. The condition of the servant – that section at least which lives in the servants' hall – may often be described as a condition of starvation in the midst of plenty. Food there is usually enough and to spare, but is it a suitable kind of food, and how is it prepared? In bygone days, the huge joint of beef, no doubt, formed the fitting fare of the burly retainers, whose duties kept them for the most part in the open air. The bumper of strong ale wrought but little harm on the man who rode to hunt or fray. The conditions of the servant's life have long since altered, but not so the manner of living, that is, so far as his food is concerned. Physiological considerations and dietetic principles have both in substance and preparation completely revolutionised the table of the master, while the servant's fare remains unchanged. The work of many men-servants is lighter than that of shopmen, and yet they are fed like navvies. What the effects of this system are, the statistics of the London hospitals will show.

The *preparation* of the food sent to the servants' hall is often grossly inadequate. The energies of the head of the kitchen department are usually absorbed by the upstairs dinner, or if not, by below-stairs social obligations. It is a principle with most cooks that they are not engaged to cook for servants; consequently the servants' hall is left to the tender mercies of the kitchenmaid, who usually does most of the cooking of the house while the responsible person receives visitors in the 'room'. The result of all this is that a huge badly cooked joint is sent to the servants' table. This appears cold again and again at a succession of suppers and dinners, till some one, nauseated at its continual reappearance, chops it up and assigns the greater part to the swill-tub. This is followed by another joint, which goes the same round and shares the same fate. Any variety beyond that of a very occasional sweet is out of the question. The physiological effects of such a dietary on those capable of assimilating it I need not point out. That those whose digestive powers are not equal to this coarse abundance must either starve or make rogues of themselves is equally obvious.

But if the coarse fare of the Middle Ages is out of place in our present-day life, there yet remains an institution still more fraught with danger. I allude to the household beer. How this pernicious practice is perpetuated passes my comprehension. The effects of ill feeding are not at first sight obvious, the effects of alcohol are clamant. One would think the shrewd employer feared the servant should emerge to true manhood, and sought to enervate and keep him malleable by this means. Hundreds of men get their first start in a drunkard's career from this hateful practice. If the youth escapes falling a victim to his gastronomic propensities he is often caught here. The claims of good fellowship, the anxiety to be thought a man, the stimulus he finds drink gives him when called upon to make a spurt, all combine to foster the habit. He is soon fit to join the ranks of the 'swill-tubs', who measure their daily consumption by the gallon. And this class we know to form no inconsiderable number of English men-servants.

Suppose, however, that a servant escapes the snares which beset him at the outset of his career. Suppose strength of character or quality of temperament enables him to steer clear of the debilitating traps laid for him, what are his chances of developing a strong and intelligent manhood? His opportunities for self-improvement are usually very small. The hours he may call his own are fitful and rare. His duties may be light, but if he wishes to prove himself a good servant he must always be on the alert. Under such circumstances fruitful application is out of the question. If he persists he must take time from his sleep, which he can often ill afford. If, again, he seeks for some society in which he may find help towards better things, he finds himself, as we have seen, surrounded by sensualists in a more or less advanced stage of degradation. If he looks abroad he finds himself shunned. He is a servant, and as the kindly world measures the individual by the type, it will have none of him. Help he has none, and he passes through life cursing the circumstances that placed him in domestic service. The higher qualities in a servant are decidedly at a discount. To methodically perform certain stereotyped duties in a stereotyped manner is in service the highest virtue. Whether the agent is drunk or is sober, has a soul or has not, is seldom taken into account. Any departure from certain conventional rules is sternly repressed, and yet, if an emergency finds him unprepared to take the initiative, he is sworn at for his incapacity.

There is still another way in which the better class of servant is hampered in his struggle for manhood. The fact that outsiders look down on servants as belonging to an inferior and degraded class has already been alluded to. In this they only take the cue from the servants' employers, who never fail to make it known, both at home and abroad, how much they despise those fellow-creatures whose misfortune it is to have to perform for them certain duties described as menial. If this attitude of supercilious scorn is in some degree justifiable, it is at least inconsistent, for it is most often adopted by those whose title to contempt in the abstract is much clearer than that of their servants.

However, this practice of emphasising superior merit by perpetually reminding the servant of his inferiority exists, and it is extremely trying to the more deserving servant. Duties which in the nature of things he would, and which he could very efficiently perform, are passed over him as beyond his abilities or as affording a test his integrity cannot stand. If in any difficulty he ventures to make a suggestion, he at once evokes a more or less direct reminder of his position. A careful conning of his weekly book and a critical surveillance of the monthly bills convince him that he is not trusted. If he is a butler he has the wine put out for him in driblets, and in every way his unfitness for any real responsibility is emphasised. This, of course, is not felt by the average servant who recognises it as his due, and, like the dog for his thrashing, he is obsequiously grateful. It is, however, extremely galling to a good man to find his master refuse him the confidence which he readily accords to his clerk. Treatment of the kind described unfortunately does not end with outraged feeling. There is nothing more readily makes a rogue of a man than systematic distrust. If a butler is given out six bottles of wine, he can by careful manipulation have one for himself. If his stores are measured out to him in handfuls, he can easily represent that he uses more than he does. If the man does not at once sink to these practices under such a *régime*, it is generally only a matter of time. The treatment he experiences saps his self-respect, and by-and-by he comes to think of himself as his master thinks. He argues that he is not trusted, therefore there can be no breach of confidence in taking all he can get. He does not care a straw for the wine or the stores, but he learns to take a pleasure in showing that his would-be clever master can be 'done'.

I think it will be seen that the conditions of life in domestic service are such as would tend to produce the very results we find. And yet the complaints we hear about servants are based on the assumption that the servants themselves are entirely responsible for their shortcomings. Employers see their servants surrounded with temptations and debasing influences to an extent unknown in other walks of life, and expect them to be free from vice. They require them to perform certain duties which involve the loss of freedom and opportunity for moral and intellectual improvement, and then complain of inefficiency and stupidity. They treat their servants as immoral, they unnecessarily limit their exercise of responsibility, they frown on any spontaneous action which does not fall in with their own caprice, and then look for the development of high moral character.

If employers really wish for improvement amongst their servants, it lies for the most part with themselves to effect the change. They must first of all put a stop to that wasteful and noxious license which I have the best reason to believe goes on in at least six houses out of every ten. At the same time they must see that their servants are provided with well-prepared food, adapted to the work they have to perform. As matters stand, the servant must either gorge himself with half-cooked meat, or steal what he can from the upstairs table, or starve. This kind of thing ought not to be. Those who keep servants ought to see that the conditions of life are healthful, both physically and morally. The practice of giving beer, too, ought to be abolished in every house in the kingdom. If employers once realised the amount of disgusting animalism this habit perpetuated they would stop it at once. They cannot, however, of themselves readily find out the real state of affairs, and many who do find out do not trouble. The domestic servants' duties make so little demand upon the faculties that when once a mechanical habit has been formed they are as well done by a man in a besotted condition as when sober.

No doubt changes like those proposed would involve trouble, but why should not trouble be taken? The *laissez faire* policy is far too prevalent in dealings with servants when the discharge of duties is not in question. Society is too much taken up with its balls and millinery, its dinners and matchmaking, ever to think of its duties towards dependants. The care of servants is too often relegated to a butler or housekeeper more debauched than those over whom they have charge. They possess neither the strength of character nor the tact required to rule others, for they have never learned to rule themselves. They manage by such extraneous aids as assuming the title of 'Mr' and 'Mrs' and retiring to the sacred precincts of the 'room' to procure a little show of respect, which most often veils the heartfelt contempt of their subordinates. Responsibilities so serious should be attended to first hand, or, if they must be discharged vicariously, it should be seen that really competent persons were set to such a task.

Advertisements for housemaids in *The Times*, 31 August 1880.

'Servants of the Wrong Sort: Sketches from Life by a Sufferer – The Selfish One'. (*The Graphic*, 21 December 1878)

'Servants of the Wrong Sort: Sketches from Life by a Sufferer – I Heard the Crash.' (*The Graphic*, 21 December 1878)

'Servants of the Wrong Sort: Sketches from Life by a Sufferer – Suggestive to Visitor.' (*The Graphic*, 21 December 1878)

'Servants of the Wrong Sort: Sketches from Life by a Sufferer – Everyone Has Their Own Ways.' (*The Graphic*, 21 December 1878)

'A Lesson in Washing: Housewifery Lessons Under the London School Board.' (*Illustrated London News*, 4 March 1893)

'Washing: Housewifery Lessons Under the London School Board.' (*Illustrated London News*, 4 March 1893)

'Ironing: Housewifery Lessons Under the London School Board.' (*Illustrated London News*, 4 March 1893)

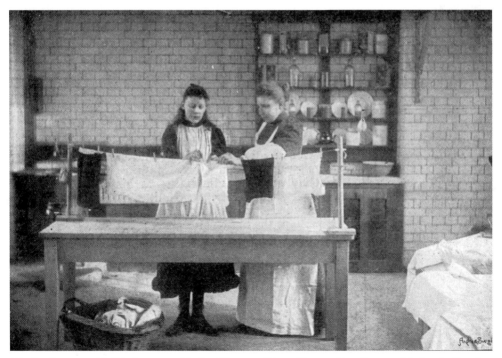

'Drying Lesson with Kindergarten Clothes, Posts and Pegs: Housewifery Lessons Under the London School Board.' (*Illustrated London News*, 4 March 1893)

Indoor servants preparing food, Patshull Hall, Patshull photographed by Bennett Clarke, circa 1900. (*Pattingham Local History and Civic Society*)

A group of servants at The Birches, Wolverhampton Road, Codsall, 1901. (*Codsall and Bilbrook Local History Society: donor and Boulton Paul Aircraft Association: creator*)

SMOKING CONCERT AT A SERVANTS' CLUB (ST. PAUL'S, KNIGHTSBRIDGE).

'A Smoking Concert at a Servants' Club', St Paul's, Knightsbridge. (*Living London*, 1901)

Postcard of domestic staff in an unidentified kitchen, circa 1905. (*Author's collection*)

Alice Eleanor Furman (seated) who got revenge on her mistress with a box of beetles. (*With thanks to Lindsay Hall*)

Cis (Bertha) Parker, who enjoyed working for the Cadbury family. (*With thanks to Hilary Donaldson*)

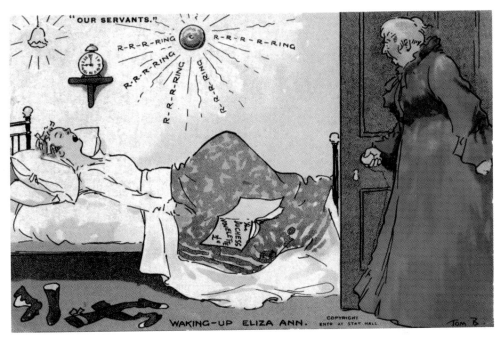

Postcard of 'Waking up Eliza Ann' by Tom Browne, postmarked 1907. (*Author's collection*)

Postcard of the 'Servants' Insurance Act', circa 1911. (*Author's collection*)

Postcard of 'The Servant Problem: At the Registry Office', circa 1910. (*Author's collection*)

Postcard of 'The Servant Question No. 6' advertising 'Quicklits', postmarked 1905. (*Author's collection*)

Postcard inscribed 'To my dear Glyn, from your Grandma's maid Ada', circa 1905. (*Author's collection*)

Postcard of an unidentified footman, circa 1905. (*Author's collection*)

Morning wear for a parlourmaid.
(*Cassell's Household Guide*, 1911)

Afternoon wear for a parlourmaid.
(*Cassell's Household Guide*, 1911)

Postcard inscribed 'Maggie, our maid 1916'. Maggie is dressed for war work. (*Author's collection*)

Reflected Sunlight

The charm and health-giving properties of a room flooded with sunlight are enormously increased and an added beauty attained by a well-polished floor; the discerning eye, too, is unconsciously delighted with its myriad pleasing reflections.

MANSION POLISH

quickly gives a fascinating polish to Parquet and Stained Wood Floors and preserves Linoleum.

In tins 6d., 10½d. and 1/9. Large household tin, containing 2 lbs. net, 3/-

 MIN FOR THE PIANO AND ALL HIGHLY - POLISHED SURFACES

Tins 6d. and 1/-

If your supplier does not stock, please write: Chiswick Products, Ltd., Chiswick, London, W.4

Advertisement for Mansion Polish for well-polished floors (*Punch*, 30 July 1930)

WANTED, in small house, clean, respectable Girl for kitchen; housemaid kept.—Reply by letter to Fair Mile, Longford, Gloucester. 1934

WANTED, Cook-General, age about 30; references; two in family; good wages; house parlourmaid kept.—Mrs. Vizard, Woodmancote, Court, Dursley. 1846

COMPANION-HELP Wanted, domesticated, for farmhouse; small family; Gloucestershire.—Apply Mrs. T. A .Powell, Upton Court, near Ross. 1837

WANTED, Girl (15) to assist with housework; state wages; reference required.—Muir, Huntley, Glos. 1839

WANTED, good Cook-General; help given.— Write in full 3094, Citizen, Stroud.

WANTED, at once, experienced Housemaid, 25 to 30.—Write Mrs. Bellhouse, Cotswold Grange, Cheltenham. 6969

RELIABLE General, plain cooking, male or female; family two; £1 weekly.—Write 2379, Citizen, Newnham.

GENERAL Wanted, young housemaid kept; some knowledge of cooking; good references required.—Homend Lodge, Ledbury. 1806

WANTED, experienced Cook and House-Parlourmaid for Harrow, near London; good wages given.—Apply Mrs. D'Arcy Fisher, Pendock, Tewkesbury. 2380

COOK-GENERAL, age 22 to 30, good references essential; three in family; house-parlourmaid kept; previous change in 1916.—Write Miss Workman, Woodchester Lodge, near Stroud. 3093

NURSERY Governess Wanted, ladies' family, £45; state experience, when free.—5, Sea View Terrace, Weston-super-Mare. 1807

MARRIED Couple required, family two, butler and cook; salary £100.—Write particulars "Cayuga," Uphill, Weston-super-Mare. 1808

WANTED, Daily Girl or Woman, able to do plain cooking.—Apply after 6 p.m. Mrs. Harding, Rockleigh, Butter-row Hill, Stroud. 3100

COOK-GENERAL, with some experience, for September 15th.—Mrs. Bruce, Sunnycroft, Tuffley. 2352

'Situations Vacant' in the *Gloucester Citizen*, 29 July 1926 (*From The British Newspaper Archive www. britishnewspaperarchive.co.uk. Image © Local World Limited. Image created courtesy of THE BRITISH LIBRARY BOARD*)

There is another aspect under which the changes suggested would be more likely to commend themselves to the employers of servants. I have no hesitation in saying that there are hundreds of houses in the country where, if the superfluity of animal food was to be taken away contemporaneously with the introduction of rational management, the butcher's bill might be reduced by one-half. The amount spent on beer, which at present is money worse than wasted, would mean a considerable saving. This, to a struggling country squire, would be no small matter. In this connection I may say that in three out of the five houses in which I have lived during the last fourteen years there was a regular system of disposing of the stale lumps of meat that were sent to the servants' table. While deploring the circumstances which led to it, it was impossible to help sympathising with the servants in this proceeding, in which they seemed only to be following the natural instinct of self-preservation.

It will, however, be little use to remove the obstacles which lie in the way of the servant's material well-being unless there be given him at the same time some opportunity for mental improvement. The servant is, as a rule, far less well-informed than any class in the same plane of life. His inability to talk on any subject, unless perhaps horse-racing or the latest music-hall attraction, is well known. This is primarily due to the low kind of life he is forced to lead, and in a less degree to the want of opportunity for self-improvement and social intercourse. The paralysing influence of the servants' environment has prevented his calling very loudly for more freedom. It does not, however, follow that because he does not ask for it should not be given him. Employers of labour believe that the stimulus and friendly rivalry offered by clubs and social meetings tend to increase the efficiency of the hands, and accordingly they voluntarily promote, and even support, such institutions. Something of the kind, on the lines indicated by Lady Aberdeen, ought to be encouraged. If, moreover, a little more liberty and opportunity for profitable social intercourse were to be granted, one of the drawbacks which prevent a better class from going to service would be taken away. Thus agencies would be set to work by which, both from within and without the standard of character and efficiency would be raised; a result which could not fail to be welcome to the employer.

With the evolution of a better class of servant, however, there must be a change in the attitude of the master. He does not scruple nowadays to act towards a man of high moral character as though he were a rogue or a thief. He forgets that the servant whom he treats like a dog may have nerves as highly strung, and may feel as acutely as the guest whom he must treat with courtesy. The amount of refined cruelty that is perpetrated upon servants by employers and their families cannot be told. There are some persons described as ladies and gentlemen who deliberately make use of their superior knowledge for the purpose of giving pain to those of their servants whom a flaw in their character or some shortcoming has placed at the mercy of their diabolical arts. I have in my mind's eye a lady (?) who conducted prayer meetings for women in her house, who habitually addressed the servants of the household as though they were brute beasts. When she allowed an opportunity for getting a servant into trouble pass (which she rarely did), she always apprised the culprit of her forbearance. I have known this person escape censure at the expense of a servant who, standing by, was gentleman enough to withhold his story (which was convincing), in order that the creature should escape. I mention this case in particular, because the lady always appeared to me in the light of a psychological problem, inasmuch as she was considered an angel by the women among whom she worked. Possibly the building up of a reputation for sanctity upon the basis of fallen human nature involved a strain which could only be relieved by at times letting the Old Adam have his way. Anyhow, it was bad for the scapegoats.

No doubt the enervation of the servant by the causes mentioned in the earlier parts of this paper has done much to expose him to harsh treatment. It is, however, unjustifiable, and it has been shown to be disastrous to the servant of better character. It is the distrust, the nagging and worry of domestic service, which perhaps more than anything else drives men to get away from it as soon as they can. And it is indeed hard that, after giving up the best years of his life to service, he should be driven to invest his savings in some business for which he has had absolutely no training, and in which in 50 per cent of cases he is doomed to failure. Surely domestic service might be made so that a man could end his days in it with some approach to comfort! Intrinsically there is nothing in service of which a man need be ashamed. There is nothing derogatory to a man's dignity or self-respect in the discharge of its humblest duties. But the thorn lies in the fact that a man, for peace sake, is reduced to a kind of degrading sycophancy; or, to use a phrase common among servants, 'he cannot call his soul his own'.

Let the conditions of domestic service be improved, and with improved conditions let the standard for the performance of duties be raised. Put service more on a level with a trade; let better service be required; but let the servant be treated as a man. In this way the existing corruption would be abolished, and the abuses servants now complain of be a thing of the past. The place of so many ciphers would be taken by men, a state of things which would inevitably revert to the well-being of society at large.

Part III

1900–1914

Edwardian Domestic Service

I am very often shut right indoors from one week to another, Tuesday to Tuesday I never have a day out; my mistress will not be inconvenienced so far. I consider all maids should have two hours each day to call their own, with the option of going out or remaining in the house ... Domestic service would not be nearly such a monotonous occupation if a little variation were included. A good home and good food is not all that is required by servants.

(A servant who completed a questionnaire for the C. V. Butler report on *Domestic Service: An Enquiry by the Women's Industrial Council* in 1913.)

As the nineteenth century passed and the twentieth began, there was no dawning of a new age for servants. However, Edwardian maids would prove even more exacting about working and living conditions than their Victorian counterparts, and the gradual shift away from domestic service among working-class women continued. The 'servant problem' debate persisted, now focusing on the scarcity rather than quality of servants, as it became increasingly difficult for employers to find domestics.

Census figures bear this out: there was a definite slowdown in the growth of servant numbers, which did not keep pace with the increase in population. In 1901, 1,330,783 female servants were recorded in England and Wales, accounting for 40 per cent of all employed women. However, ten years later, the number had only risen to 1,359,359 (around 36 per cent).

The market forces of supply and demand compelled mistresses to adjust the pay and living conditions they were offering, in order to attract quality candidates. In advertisements, employers highlighted generous holiday provision, the size of the family in the household, whether or not other servants were kept and sometimes, for how long other members of staff had been employed there. The phrase 'No washing' was almost universal by 1900, because servants were simply unwilling to do the laborious 'big wash'; families sent out their washing to laundries instead. In the cities, 'no basement' featured heavily in advertisements, as there were increasing concerns about the health of servants forced to toil day and night in basements without access to sunlight or fresh air, after *The Lancet* waded in to the debate. The phrase 'no windows' was also common, since the washing of outside windows by female servants was now discouraged too.

Newspaper advertisements remained a popular way for servants to find a new place. As one newspaper proclaimed in 1909, 'The Servant Problem is not solved yet; but you can always find a capable country girl by advertising in the *Northampton Mercury*.' Girls from the countryside were still preferred to those from towns, since there was a feeling that they were not yet tainted by talk of trade unions or excessive demands for higher pay and better working conditions. Job advertisements could still be misleading, however. Doris Hailwood was born in Shropshire around 1900. After being orphaned very young, Doris was turned out by her older sisters to fend for herself at the age of 11. Having encountered exploitation in her first two jobs in service, she was determined to find something better. She happened to glance at a newspaper while lighting her employer's fire and noticed an advert in the 'Wanted' column. It read:

> *Wanted, strong girl aged 14 to 16 years of age, skilled in housecraft and used to children to be a 'Mother's help'. Live in. Have own room and one day off in a fortnight. Wages £25 a year paid after one full year has been worked.*

Doris applied for and got the job but to her sorrow, she was just a drudge, working from 6 am to 8 pm and constantly at the beck and call of every member of the family. There were eight of them altogether, including six children, aged four to 12. Doris was only 13 years old herself. For this hard work, she received poor food and slept in a lumber room so full of junk that she barely had enough room to stretch out.

A newspaper advertisement could also lead to a gem of a job. After a succession of other posts, Doris moved to the north of England and became housekeeper, children's nurse and general factotum to a Jewish family called Jacobs. The advertisement had offered much more pay and weekly time off than any of her previous jobs, but it was also an onerous post and something of a gamble for Doris to take on. Yet, it began an association that would endure until her marriage. The Jacobs were very generous and kind, helping Doris to feel like a member of the family. Her work carried responsibility, security and a feeling of belonging she never forgot.

However, Doris's early experiences of domestic service led her to comment in later years that she was glad domestic service was in decline, considering the way that many servants, like her, had been treated. After she got married, Doris vowed that she would never allow her children to go into service.

In an attempt to solve the 'servant problem', labour-saving products and devices such as gas cookers, telephones and vacuum cleaners were introduced but uptake was very slow. Labour was still relatively cheap and it was far more expensive to install gas or pipe hot water to the bathrooms than it was to employ servants to light fires and carry hot water. Maids were still a necessity because, as E. S. Turner points out in *What the Butler Saw*, 'the most important labour-saving device of all was still lacking: a sensibly designed house.'

Much of the arduous nature of domestic service for general servants and housemaids was caused by the need to constantly fill and carry coal scuttles for fires; to haul hot water for basins and baths up numerous flights of stairs; and to remove candle wax, coal dust and soot from every surface. It was not surprising that the new two-storey villas springing up in the suburbs were so attractive to servants, since they offered a much lighter workload.

Unlike other industries, which had been the subject of government investigations, domestic service remained unregulated because it was based on a contract between two private individuals. As a result, servants' unions had been unable to make much headway in effecting change.

Jessie Stephen worked in domestic service as a 'general' and she was also involved in founding a domestic workers' union in Glasgow before the First World War. When she was interviewed about her life in 1977, Jessie described one of the homes in which she had worked:

There were four [servant] girls ... [and] they had two bathrooms [in the house] but we weren't allowed to use the bath. Oh, no! We had to go in the wash-house and have our bath in the copper, warm the water and get in the copper, one of the girls holding the door so any of the men who might pass couldn't get in. It was humiliation that servants had to suffer back then, as if we were different creatures. We were often very much cleaner than they were because we were always taught to be clean. Every one of us had a bath every week, my Mother saw to that.

This Glasgow servants' union was marginally successful:

We got two hours off every day for our members' free time because we used to only get one afternoon or evening a week and every second Sunday. We demanded that all uniform should be paid for by the employer because we didn't see why we should be paying for our uniform out of our wages every month. And oh, we made a lot of progress. We even went to the Earl of Mar's place near Dollar and we got his maids in. It was very difficult, it's like clerical workers in one or two offices. It's when you get into the big combinations that you make progress, I found when you get in the big houses we did better than in the small ones.

The problem was that most servants worked in smaller households and so, unless employers were progressive or receptive to reform, it was rare for 'union conditions' to be offered. Jessie Stephen described a place she secured through the employment agency of the Domestic Workers' Union in London:

I went to a place in Purley where I had union conditions. I had a lovely bedroom, properly furnished, and there were two teenage daughters and the man was a bank manager. So they were good middle-class stock. They would come into my kitchen and talk to me and help me if they could. I really enjoyed working in that place. I stayed there until they had to move to Herne Bay, he'd got a more important job ... That was the first job I ever had that I really enjoyed. (Recorded interview from LSE Library's collections, ref: 8SUF/B/157, 1 July 1977.)

The Domestic Workers' Union of Great Britain and Ireland was founded in 1910 and the Glasgow Union became affiliated to it. In practical terms, all the unions could do was air the servants' grievances, set up their own registry offices and provide accommodation for those who found themselves suddenly out of a place. They could not get the law changed to make it legally binding for employers to provide characters, since the government would not back any move that would interfere with the relationship between servant and employer. Low wages and long hours were another thorny topic which seemed impossible to resolve.

Ironically, two pieces of government legislation that were not specifically aimed at domestic servants would most significantly improve their lives by granting them a degree of security: the landmark Old Age Pensions Act and the National Insurance Bill.

From 1 January 1909, any eligible person over the age of 70 (including domestic servants) could benefit from the first state pension introduced under the Old Age Pensions Act. If their income was less than 8s a week, then they were entitled to a non-contributory pension of 5s per week. There was a reduced pension for those with an income of between 8s and 12s per week, but anyone with a higher income than this received nothing. Applicants who had claimed poor relief in the previous two years were also excluded.

Pensions arranged for servants by their employers were rare, unless they were long-serving members of staff in a very wealthy household, in which case they might be granted an annuity. The vast majority, however, had to fend for themselves. For ex-servants who were eligible, the new pension was a very welcome addition to their limited incomes, and doubtless helped to keep many out of the workhouse in their old age.

Charities offering limited support to elderly servants already existed such as The Domestic Servants' Benevolent Institution, which was founded in 1846 as a direct response to the large numbers of destitute elderly servants who were becoming workhouse inmates. According to Pamela Horn in *The Rise and Fall of the Victorian Servant*, in 1871 at Kensington Poor Law Infirmary 'fifty-five of the 130 female inmates recorded in the census were domestic servants; and at St George's Workhouse, Hanover Square, there were 133 female domestic servants out of a total of 434 female inmates'. For servants who had reached the end of their working lives without being able to put by sufficient savings for their retirement, the new Old Age Pension was a godsend.

The 1911 National Insurance Bill guaranteed manual workers sickness benefit and free medical treatment, and domestic servants were included in the legislation. Female servants were entitled to 7s 6d for 26 weeks if they became ill, plus free medical treatment and a disablement benefit of 5s a week, if they still could not work after 26 weeks had passed. Both employer and female servant contributed 3d a week to the scheme. With the servant's contribution, the employer bought stamps to stick on an insurance card. Male servants paid a slightly higher contribution of 4d a week, in return for a guaranteed 10s a week sickness benefit for 26 weeks.

There was great opposition to the National Insurance Bill, however, from both servants and employers, who were outraged that the government should seek to undermine the private relationship between them. Many maids did not understand the implications of the legislation and were misinformed about its benefits, while some employers felt insulted by the Bill, believing that it implied they did not look after their servants when they were ill. Sadly, in the majority of cases, this was true.

The Times (29 November 1911) reported on a deputation to Lloyd George, Chancellor of the Exchequer at the time, which consisted of representatives from various women's organisations, including the National Union of Women

Workers and the Girls' Life Brigade. They were concerned about the impact of the proposed National Insurance Bill on servants. A Charity Organisation Society official had told the president of the Girls' Life Brigade that:

> *nearly 70 per cent of the cases dealt with in his town were those of young general servants who sought aid because they were ill and had spent all their savings. Servants went to him and said they had been as long as 14 years in one place, and yet in not one case had the society got a subscription from the mistress towards the maintenance of her old servant.*

Another member of the deputation, Lady Digby, pointed out that 'however good and kind a mistress was, it was impossible for her to keep a girl in her house for more than a few days in the event of sickness or to provide for her nursing. The size of the house and the expense would entirely prevent it. Unless befriended by some society, those girls were invariably sent either to the workhouse infirmary or to a poor home.' Although the expense of 3d a week was a high sum for a young servant earning low wages, a large number of servants were already paying sums varying from 2d to 6d a week to benefit clubs or friendly societies, which very often only provided for funeral expenses.

Before the National Insurance Bill, most decent mistresses would have paid their own doctor to attend a sick servant. However, if the illness lingered on, it was not affordable for middle-class employers to keep a place open for the maid while paying for temporary help. There was little choice but to dismiss the servant and look for another; this happened to Amy Grace Rose, who was working as a nursemaid at a vicarage near Cambridge when she caught flu in about 1900. Some mistresses did find places for servants who had been weakened by illness, and needed a position with lighter work. In spite of the opposition, the legislation was passed in 1911, coming into effect in July 1912, and the 'stamp' became part and parcel of domestic service.

An excellent barometer to feelings about pre-war domestic service on the part of both servants and employers can be found in Violet (C. V.) Butler's report, *Domestic Service: An Enquiry by the Women's Industrial Council*. Although this report was not published until 1916, the questionnaires on which it was based were completed by maids and mistresses in the summer of 1913. There were 708 replies from employers and 566 from servants, plus hundreds of letters, which were sent either privately or through the press from employers and workers. According to the writers of the report, a large proportion of the answers were 'long and careful and eminently human documents'. This was perhaps the first time that the personal opinions of servants had been officially sought on such a scale, and they were eager to have their say.

The enquiry sought to determine the conditions in domestic service as an industry and to ascertain what kind of general improvements could be made. This was, the authors stated, because between 'the violent malcontents who have suffered from exceptionally bad mistresses or maids, and the type which is "always happy" and aloof from the path of reform, there is a very large class whose relationship is not satisfactory and whose mutual jars are partly responsible for the constant undersupply of servants.'

The servants' voices leap off the page. 'A good cook and an abstainer', with wages £30 to £35, wrote that she had a few hours off one afternoon a week, but had to cook late dinners on Sundays. She continued:

I am sorry to say I have no other trade I could do; I should be only too pleased to say good-bye to domestic service. We can only describe it as prison without committing a crime ... No, if a girl has brains, by all means let her make use of them; the less brains she has in service, the more she can stand the insults from her superiors, so unless she is naturally dull, put her to something more interesting ... Every trade has its compulsory hours, but the poor servant is left entirely to the mistress to treat her as she feels, sometimes not very kindly. Why not shorten her hours, or make the wages hourly, but it must and should be compulsory. Why should not we have time for other things besides work? They should be compelled to let us out once on the Sabbath, and long enough to go a distance ...

Service in its present state is serious, and if something is not done soon I am afraid it will be the lower class, not the refined girl of years ago that tries service. Ladies will see the difference. They are themselves entirely to blame, we that have had good training always respect our betters when we meet them. I have often wished I could have learned shorthand and typewriting, also dressmaking and millinery, as I think these occupations would have helped one to pass off the monotony of domestic service ... Service would be better if domestics were given a little more time in which to do as they liked, not to feel tied to answer bells or watch over the cooking, or the other odds and ends that take so much time. If they were to have a time each day away from these things, or to be allowed to have visitors more often, it would lessen the monotony of service a good deal ... I think most girls in service would agree with me that we ought to be allowed a little more time for outdoor exercise, as time and work begin to drag heavily when one does not go out for a week, perhaps, when it is your Sunday in.

With regard to the strict rules to be followed as a servant, a hard–worked housemaid, earning £24, wrote:

> *A great thing against domestic service is the rule, "no followers allowed". Ladies are quite right in not allowing young men to their houses whom they know nothing about, but supposing a girl has been keeping company with a young man whom she can only see for a few hours three times a fortnight, that is, alternate Sundays and one evening a week, what can she know of his habits, likes and dislikes in home life, if she only sees him when he puts on his best manners. He might be entirely different from what one judges him to be; and if they should marry it might lead to unhappiness and disappointment. If ladies are doubtful about their maids' sweethearts, they could enquire about their characters at their employers'. There are many ways in which they could find out if a young man is honest or not.*

The writers of the report discovered that little had changed since the late Victorian period and significantly, that:

> *lack of liberty ... remains the expressed or unexpressed grievance in the majority of cases. To some extent it is inherent in domestic service, and is a necessary exchange for the greater comfort obtainable and for the sheltered life. It is for the individual to estimate the value of the exchange.*

In order to solve the problem of inaccurate references, several employers suggested introducing 'character books' along the lines of the German system, to ensure 'a brief written record of the maid's work and conduct in each successive situation'. However, most of the mistresses surveyed did not believe this was necessary.

The idea of a system of training featured heavily in the report. It concluded that a State-controlled Central Bureau was required and this would have to go much further than the current efforts of the Labour Exchanges (which had begun offering domestic service roles at the beginning of the First World War) and servants' registry offices. Homes for girls out of employment were also suggested.

Although the C. V. Butler report was published in 1916, nothing of any significance transpired as a result of its findings, largely because the huge financial burden of the war meant there was a lack of available funds.

The Social Status of Servants

How servants saw their place in society depended very much on their experiences of domestic service and the views of those around them. If they had kind, considerate employers, then they were naturally more likely to have a positive experience. For example, Cis Parker enjoyed working for the paternalistic Cadbury family, who were genuinely concerned for her health and well-being, while Queenie Harris took pride in her work as a parlourmaid for an employer who treated her as an equal, 'not mistress and maid'.

Mary Doughty was born in 1889 near the town of Stafford, which was home to numerous shoe factories. Like many bright girls who enjoyed school, Mary was highly literate. She saw domestic service as a cut above factory work, and in later life, was always keen to stress she had been 'in service' and not a 'factory girl'. Working as a house parlourmaid for employers such as the Bostocks (one of the town's local 'shoe barons'), Mary believed that she was in a cleaner, more pleasant environment than the girls in the shoe factories. This may well have been the case because she worked for wealthy households employing two or three other servants. Mary was also proud that she had never been a chambermaid and therefore never had to 'empty the slops' (chamber pots).

Looking back on her life, she never considered herself to have been in a servile position in any way and was glad to have had the opportunity to mingle with a different sphere to that which she was born into, learning new skills such as cleaning silver and laying a formal dinner table.

A similar view was held by a cook-housekeeper with 31 years' experience of service from the age of 14:

> *I will never regret being a domestic servant. I have tried to do my duty well, and have been well rewarded for doing so. I consider that we are better off than shop-girls or factory girls: we may not have so much money for wages, but we have our board and lodging free, also washing, which is equal to 12s or 14s a week. When the shop or factory girl pays for her food and lodgings she has very little. If a girl is not well trained at home she will never make a good servant: girls now-a-days are spoiled at home; their mothers never teach them how to work.*

Contrast this with the jobbing London cook who had experienced the negative attitudes of some employers at first-hand: 'I have been in very good houses where one is treated as a human being. The better bred people, the *real* gentlefolk, do treat their employees as flesh and blood, the 'jumped up rich middle classes' *as cattle*. I have not written too strongly, because I have been through it.'

Many of the servants who completed questionnaires for the C. V. Butler report commented on the treatment they received from middle-class employers. A parlourmaid, aged 38, wrote:

> *I think service is the best thing for girls. I find if a girl does her work and duty she is well done by. No doubt there are some bad places; I myself have had two or three, but I have left at the end of a month when I have found how impossible it has been, and that is what I advise any girl to do. The only thing I complain of is the way middle-class people look down upon us; people no better, and often not so well brought up as a good servant, pass remarks like this – "Oh, she is only a servant." Then they do not want to know us, but I wish people who look down upon servants to understand that no one is so well off as a good servant.*

Charring as an Alternative

The trend towards daily charring continued. Young women and girls shunned 'live-in' domestic service because it meant that they were tied to their employers' homes and always at their beck and call. There was no such dislike of charring, however, because the hours were fixed and charladies went home at the end of the day. This type of work was often undertaken by impoverished married women who needed to supplement their husbands' scanty wages. As a result of widespread poverty in particular areas, there were always more charladies than work available, and it was very badly paid; it was also no less strenuous than live-in domestic work.

As Carl Chinn points out in *They Worked All Their Lives*, 'all charladies were characterised by the fact that they were women of the urban poor who performed the rough and arduous tasks eschewed by the better-off of society'. He describes a regular day's charring work from 9am to 3pm as consisting of 'washing and drying up the breakfast dishes; filling up the coal-scuttles from the outhouse; cleaning the fire irons with emery cloth; blackleading the fire-grate; dusting, cleaning and polishing cutlery and ornaments, and beating and shaking the carpets outside'.

The Association of Trained Charwomen had been established by the Women's Industrial Council in 1898, to give women a week's training in household work or cooking, under a certificated teacher of Domestic Economy. The Association was not a registry office but it did vet the candidates, who, it claimed, were 'selected and tested with great care'. Every member was given an engagement register in which their employers wrote and signed remarks, which formed a series of references, in line with the German system of character books. The charwomen and the employers had to adhere to strict conditions: working hours were not to exceed 10 hours a day and the wages were to be 2s 6d per day with meals or 3s 6d without.

Employers paid a small fee to use the service: 6d for an engagement of a week or less, 1s for a month, 2s 6d for six months or 5s for a year to cover all engagements with every class of worker. Unfortunately, there was never a sufficient number of employers to provide work for the ever increasing number of applicants, indicating that the convenience of live-in maids was still preferred.

Alice Eleanor Furman

General Servant and Housemaid

Born in Paddington in 1889, Alice Eleanor Furman was one of seven children. Her father was a tailor and Alice had a strict upbringing. In 1903 after leaving school at the age of 14, she went into service until she got married in 1912. The following stories of Alice's time in domestic service were told to her granddaughter, Lindsay Hall.

I left school the week of my fourteenth birthday. Over the weekend, my box was packed and on Monday I was off and into service. I had no say in the matter and my father arranged everything. This was how things were in those days and, although I did not want to leave home, I did not dare question this.

Nothing I have ever done was as hard as being a servant – at the beck and call of people who certainly considered themselves your superiors, although I had my own opinions on that. The hours were always long – up in time to lay fires by 6am and often working till late at night. Your life was not your own and there was very little time off. The worst thing was the dinner party as this meant extra work and not being able to go to bed until everything was cleared and washed up and the last guests had long departed. I remember the smart dresses of the lady guests and how there was always a large awning put up above the front door which stretched across the pavement so that the guests could leave their carriages and come into the house without getting wet.

Did I learn anything? Yes, apart from the fact that I was of little consequence, I learnt that putting halves of empty eggshells in the bottom of the coffee pot keeps the coffee clear of grounds!

At one place I worked [*possibly in West Hampstead*], I was on my own in the house except for the mistress who was actually quite a nice person and was kind to me. I was working in the kitchen when I heard loud screams coming from the parlour above, accompanied by frantic ringing of the bell. I rushed upstairs and found my employer lying on the floor in a pool of blood. She was in a very bad way but was able to explain that she had not been attacked by some villain, which was my first thought, but was suffering from severe internal bleeding and that I must get the doctor as quickly as possible. I hated to leave her in this state as she was bleeding so badly but there was no choice. Before I went, I fetched a chair and propped her legs up on it in the hope that this would slow the bleeding.

I hitched up my skirt, held onto my cap and ran like the devil was after me. I ignored the stares of people in the street. I must have bumped into a few. I was so glad that I knew where the doctor's house was and so relieved to find that he was at home. I made it known how urgent it was that he should attend the mistress and he told me to wait while he harnessed up his pony and trap. I said that I could not wait and would run back to the house. This I did and I arrived a few minutes before the doctor himself.

The mistress was still bleeding but not so badly now and between us, we got her tightly wrapped in sheets and carried her out to the doctor's trap and off to the hospital. I thought that I would not be seeing her again, but whatever they did to her in the hospital, she survived, although she had to stay in bed for weeks. I was told that I had saved her life, although I thought that anyone would have done the same but it was good to have a little bonus in my next wage packet.

In another house I worked in, the mistress was never satisfied and although other help was kept, I was the only one of the servants who was prepared to do the unpleasant job of removing the black beetles that seemed to have made their home in the house in large numbers. The mistress was terrified of them and whenever one was spied anywhere near her, she would scream, "Alice!" or "Fetch Alice!" I would have to set aside whatever I was doing at the time and rush to remove the creature, and this really got on my wick!

Sometimes when I had some rare time off, I would go out with or go to see my favourite brother, Bob. If I got back later than was allowed and found the doors locked, I would get Bob to give me a leg-up to a window which I had left partly open for the purpose. Of course, one evening we were caught in the act and although I explained that Bob was my brother and not a 'follower', I was told that I was "wicked" and that I was sacked. To be honest, I was glad to be out of there although I had to go and stay with Bob and his wife as my parents were none too pleased with me.

Don't they say that 'revenge is sweet?' On my last day, I found a small box and went around the house collecting all the black beetles I could find. I wrapped the box and addressed it to my ex-employer and sent it to her in the post. I only wished I could have seen her face when she opened it over breakfast!

Alice left domestic service when she married Joseph Perry in 1912; they had two children. After Joseph was killed during the Somme campaign in August 1916, Alice re-married in 1920 to Ernest Henry Young, a widower with a young disabled son. The family grew in 1924 when Alice and Ernest formally adopted the eldest daughter of their neighbour, who had died of tuberculosis. Alice died in 1982, aged 93.

Cis Parker

Kitchen-maid

Born Bertha May Jennings in 1893 in Walsall, Cis Parker was the daughter of a silver plater. She went into service at about the age of 16, working for the Cadbury family in Selly Oak near Birmingham. This was her only place since she stayed there until her marriage.

Cis was interviewed about her time in domestic service in May 1980. This extract comes from the recording of that interview, which is held at Walsall Local History Centre (Cis Parker 162/1/36A). It is reproduced with the permission of Walsall Local History Centre and her granddaughter, Hilary Donaldson.

My mother's cousin was housekeeper [for the Cadburys] ... she used to go and take care of the house if they was away ... They were probably away a month, they went abroad usually for their holiday. They were in touch with ... my mother's relatives ... although I didn't know them personally at that time. [When] I went there, they ... had a nice house called Westholme at Selly Oak [and] they'd got a house over in the country, you see. We used to go there part of the time. They couldn't have been kinder people.

[There were] seven on the staff. There wasn't a butler, they were teetotal, the Cadburys was. They didn't need a butler. There were seven maids, [two] chauffeurs, five gardeners; that's how big the place was but they couldn't have been kinder people to work for.

I was a kitchen-maid first, then I wasn't very well towards Christmas. Mrs Cadbury said to one of the senior maids, "Have you taken Bertha to the doctor's? I don't think she's very well." So they took me, one of the maids, [and] he said straight away, "She's working too hard." It was a big house and I wasn't very big like some people. She said, "You're not very big, you're not very strong."

So I had this milk the same as Mr Cadbury [that had] come from their farm. He put it on a cup and saucer in the pantry and it set and the cream comes to the top, you see. Also, the extra milk [and porridge], but I wasn't big enough to be a kitchen maid at that time, I grew bigger after but not much. I've never been very big.

They [first] saw me when I was 12 ... I was no bigger at 16 than I was at 12. My Aunt Bessie thought I should grow, they thought I should be as big as the others. With all the food and the attention I had to have just to please them, it sounds absolutely silly but it was the truth ... They must have liked me or they wouldn't have took me with all those against me size. They were all big hefty people but Mr Cadbury was a nice man, couldn't have been kinder.

They didn't spoil you with having so much money because it isn't wise anyway, you've got to live with the rest of the people, I don't believe in spoiling people and giving them too much money 'cause you like them. They must be trained in the proper way.

[Mrs Cadbury] said to me, "Oh, Bertha, you're far too young to go out at evening, you'll have to have your time off during the day and be back at 6 o'clock." Those were the kind of people [they were]. Me being young, I couldn't be out in the dark, [so I] wasn't allowed half a day. What Mother allowed me [to do] when I come home to Walsall was a different thing, she pleased herself, but [that was] their rules. Mrs Cadbury said, "We couldn't let you out after 6 o'clock."

My brothers were quite a lot older, ten years older than me. They used to laugh about it ... I wasn't allowed out after 6 o'clock [even though I was 16, 17] ... you'd got to be in [on] time.

[Mrs Cadbury] used to say, "Bertha, we're going away this weekend ... and you can go home if you like." One of the other girls used to come. I used to go by train [to Walsall]. I know when I first went, she wrote [down] all the trains from New Street ... I'd got to go from Selly Oak into [New Street to] change the trains. It wasn't very often that I had a lift, [although] they'd got two cars and two chauffeurs ...

On a Sunday, Mr Cadbury always used to fill a bowl of fruit, oranges and apples, and then put [in] seven bars of crème, the wrapped up Cadbury's [chocolate], and it used to be wrapped in seven pieces and you knew that was your bonus! You could get pounds then, cheap from the [factory]. [On Sundays] we used to have our time off. We used to go where we liked ... Some were Quakers, some were Catholics, they didn't mind what religion, you kept to your own. I was always Church of England and I always went to church.

We had a big room over the yard. We had three beds which we liked much better in one big room, but there was curtains between all of them. You could ... draw the curtains round to make it private. When you'd time, you'd have a chat perhaps or something like that and then the lights would be out. The senior ones had a bedroom [each] and ... there was one room at the far end [for] the head cook, my cousin – she was housekeeper. She used to have a room to herself. I used to have to light her fire so to have a nice fire ready. We had our own bathroom for the maids which was as nice as possible.

Dinner was at 8, [so] by the time you'd got all the clearing away, there wasn't any spare time. I used to go to bed at half past nine, the others went at 10. Me being young ... the lads at home used to laugh because I'd been up till 10 years ago.

They didn't go in for [big parties]. They was friendly, they were Quakers, they had more of a group of their own friends. They wouldn't have the same interests as the other people ... They might send them a subscription but they wouldn't have anything in common. They were very, very generous.

[Mr Cadbury] bought the chimes [for the new school] and they used to play four beautiful hymns in chimes in the evening, always at sunset, when the day was over. 'The day they gave us, Lord has ended'. So everyone at Bournville could hear them, like the Carillon [Bells]. It was very nice really. It was a beautiful place ... to live.

[In 1916] I was pleased to [be getting] married and I was very happy in my life. Mrs Cadbury said, "I want to see this boyfriend of yours." I was engaged, see. If you weren't engaged, you're not considered [as having] a boyfriend ...

Mrs Cadbury shook hands with him. I was marrying a miner [and] they had seen him just once, but knew very little about [him]. Mr Cadbury said to me, "Now remember, Bertha, we shall always be pleased to hear from you at any time. If you're in any difficulties ..." [Mrs Cadbury] said, "You write and let us know and we shall always be pleased to hear from you."

Exceptionally kind they were, all the Cadbury family. They were genuinely concerned about [me] ... she bought for my wedding present all my household linen, bought me everything it was possible to buy, sheets, pillow slips, all kinds, and everything as you could mention. The older ones ... they suggested to Mrs Cadbury what I liked and they were the ones as helped the choice ... [to] have what I wanted was a great thing. Some of those things I got for years ... I shall always treasure them and the memory ... [I kept] in touch with them ... for many years.

Cis married Samuel Parker in 1916 and they had four children. Samuel left the pit in around 1930 because of ill health, and Cis ran a fish and chip shop in Bloxwich for about ten years. After retiring to Short Heath, she was widowed at the age of 55, so she returned to Walsall to live with her sister Millie. Cis died in 1984.

Jessie Stephen

General Servant

Born in 1893, Jessie Stephen was the daughter of a tailor who worked for the Co-operative Society in Glasgow. When she was 14, she won a scholarship but had to leave school the following year when her father was temporarily unemployed. Jessie went into domestic service in Glasgow, yet she also became a labour activist at an early age; she was made vice-president of the Maryhill branch of the Independent Labour Party at the age of 16. She was also a militant suffragette and a member of the Women's Social and Political Union, who dropped acid into pillar boxes while wearing her maid's uniform.

Wanting to improve the lot of domestic servants, in 1913, Jessie founded a servants' union in Glasgow. Although there were minor successes, it was difficult to recruit members and the union eventually became affiliated to the Domestic Workers' Union of Great Britain.

This extract is taken from an article Jessie wrote for *The Sunday Post* (11 May 1919) entitled 'My Experiences as a Maid':

Although in its infancy, the Domestic Servants' Union can boast of 4000 members with large branches in London and Glasgow. You can ready understand I feel proud of the result, because domestics offer quite a number of difficulties that do not present themselves in the organisation of the ordinary industrial worker.

The problem of getting the right type of girl for domestic service was never so acute as at the present juncture. The reason is not far to seek. At the outbreak of war many girls, on patriotic grounds, left their household duties, and went out to help the country in its time of need. Some entered munition factories in the great industrial nerve centres of the country, others rallied to the call of the Red Cross, while hundreds undertook work in the public services in order to relieve men for the army. Now, all these spheres were entirely different from anything to which the average domestic had been accustomed. In these spheres the average girl widened her outlook, enjoyed a new sense of liberty, and, moreover, received a scale of remuneration hitherto unknown to her. Can you wonder, then, that she has no desire to return to the kitchen under the old conditions?

In the past the domestic servant worked long hours, received comparatively small wages, and experienced no sense of liberty comparable with other women workers. Even in some of the best "places" capable servants were compelled to occupy living-rooms that were a disgrace to modern civilisation.

Take my own case. My bedroom was in the basement of a West End flat. There was a tar macadam floor, covered here and there by a few fragments of carpet that betrayed manifest signs of senile decay. The place was as cheerless as the grave. In another, where the family was of good social standing, my room was also in the basement, but the bed was in a cupboard. I couldn't get a chair into the apartment, and the door provided the only means of ventilation.

There I lived on the fat of the land! What! One luscious kipper was divided between the cook and your humble servant. On certain days we were allowed an egg on the same principle. During the cook's absence on one occasion, I was called upon to scramble six eggs for the entire household, and, my share being included, it did not go far to satisfy a perfect digestion. In the same house margarine at 6d per lb was ordered for the kitchen, and the best butter for upstairs. Sometimes the order was reversed, and then a long complaint from the mistress was directed to the grocer!

In one of these places I had the honour on several occasions of working for fourteen to twenty hours at a spell.

For a time I was employed in a big establishment where the mistress was very religious and highly distinguished for philanthropy. Here the hours were long, the wages poor, and the work arduous. One fine day I resolved to ask an increase of two shillings per month. After dinner one evening I met the mistress and made my request.

Judge of my surprise when she informed me that she would pray to the Lord about the matter, and let me know in the morning. When I interviewed her next day, she informed me quite frankly that she had meditated and prayed about my request, but could not see her way to grant the increase. I politely inquired why she always put the onus upon the Lord when the servants desired an increase in wages, and with all her accustomed dignity she lectured me for being so blasphemous and flippant. I assured her it was she who was blasphemous, and that the Lord had little conception of the conditions under which her servants were working, otherwise her conscience would disturb her sleep oftener than it did. The mistress was very much grieved at my outburst, and particularly so when I informed her I was about to leave. Within two months, I obtained a post at double the salary. When I was about to walk out, this very religious lady would have done anything to retain me.

During the war we have discovered many things. The fierce light of public opinion has been focused upon many social sores. The domestic servant's lot is one of them, and it is about to be treated.

Ladies who have a reputation for doing well by their maids are out for reform, and from these I have already received hearty support.

People who have been in the habit of keeping a little "general" and working her to death on starvation wages, must now do their own household duties, or come into line with modern requirements.

Some very accomplished girls are to be found among the better-equipped domestic servants, many of whom are infinitely more capable to manage a house than some of the mistresses. My organisation is out to train the girls, and to see that the maids recommended are efficient and reliable. In a short time we hope to solve the present registry difficulty, to open training hostels, in which we shall pay Trades Union rate of wages to the girls during the period of training. We shall charge a fee of 2s 6d for registration to mistresses, but only after they have been suited.

Domestic servants, too, must have a shorter working day. Maids must have two hours off every day, a half-day off once a week and a half-day off on Sunday, together with set times for meals.

In all the big centres we propose to open clubs for domestic servants. To these they will be at liberty to invite their lady and gentlemen friends. This side of the work we are anxious to develop, because many maids spend their days in loneliness and drudgery, and this must end if the best type of girl is to be attracted to domestic service.

In London, Jessie worked for various women's rights organisations, including the Workers' Suffrage Federation, the Ministry of Reconstruction and the National Federation of Women Workers. In later years, she became a journalist and ran her own secretarial agency. She was a lifelong trade union activist until she died in 1979, at the age of 86.

Part IV

1914–1950

The Impact of War

The War accentuated the [servant] problem and precipitated the crisis by widening the scope of women's activities while, in addition to this, many of those who had been previously employed in domestic work found the comradeship, definite hours and routine of factory, office or shop life very much to their liking, and had no desire to return to their former occupation.

(*Report of the Committee Appointed to Inquire into the Present Conditions as to the Supply of Female Domestic Servants*, 1923.)

With the outbreak of the First World War in 1914, the definition of what constituted women's work was destined to change forever. An estimated 400,000 male and female servants left domestic service for the armed forces and various areas of wartime production, as well as clerical and support services. Maids suddenly had new opportunities to undertake war work offering higher pay and greater freedom – and they were eager to take advantage of these roles.

Women frequently worked in jobs previously carried out by skilled or semi-skilled men. They found employment as land girls, nurses and bus conductresses, and in shops, canteens and offices. According to John Stevenson in *British Society 1914–1945*, the wages of typists 'were reported to have almost doubled by September 1915 from £1 to 35s per week'. From spring 1915, women also had the option of working in the munitions factories, where they could earn over £2 (40 shillings) a week. By contrast, in 1907, the average annual salaries offered in job advertisements in *The Times* were £20 13s 4d for a housemaid, £26 8s for a parlourmaid and £19 10s for a general servant.

Male servants were expected to enlist for war service, providing they were medically fit and under the maximum age limit. On the large country estates, most men-servants left to fight for King and country, but *Country Life* (January 1915) felt called upon to prick the conscience of any households still employing male staff: 'Have you a Butler, Groom, Chauffeur, Gardener or Gamekeeper serving you who, at this moment, should be serving your King and Country? ...

A great responsibility rests on you. Will you sacrifice your personal convenience for your Country's need? Ask your men to enlist TO-DAY.'

Normal life continued during the war, with the same woes for servants as they had experienced since Victorian times. Misrepresentation about the nature of roles and the workload continued, and this deception was not confined to newspaper advertisements. Employers were also less than forthcoming when it came to supplying accurate information about their vacancies for registry offices.

A servant signing herself 'Disgusted' wrote to the *Liverpool Echo* (8 February 1915) about this issue:

> *Is it not high time that something should be done in regard to "ladies" going to registry offices, and misrepresenting the situations they are offering? I was introduced at a local registry to a lady who required a temporary cook. In the course of conversation, I was told that owing to the war they were living very plainly, but I was not informed that I was expected to eat margarine for breakfast, lunch, tea and supper, else have the alternative of dry bread, with a little variation of dry toast. Two new maids arrived whilst I was there, both from a distance. They were told that owing to this terrible war high wages were not given, but as it was such an easy and most healthy place it would be more of a holiday than work. If incessant waiting upon people from 6.30 in the morning until 10pm is considered a holiday, I wonder what they will call work?*

This type of treatment, and the long hours involved, naturally made women who had been employed in war work reluctant to return to domestic service.

Post-war Domestic Service

After the war, many women who had occupied men's pre-war roles were expected to vacate their posts for returning servicemen, but having had a taste of professional independence, they were loath to adopt the shackles of service again. It was increasingly difficult for employers, except the very rich, to find and retain good servants.

Following the First World War, the average age of domestic servants increased considerably, especially in the over 35 age group. As Pamela Horn points out in *Life Below Stairs in the Twentieth Century*, in 1911, 20.5 per cent of maids in England and Wales were aged over 35, yet two decades later this had grown to 33.2 per cent. This shift had several implications for the employers:

older servants were less biddable and more likely to protest about poor living conditions or excessively long hours.

These older servants were also more expensive to employ than the young school-leavers, who had made up a third of domestics in 1911. Small middle-class households, which had previously employed these young girls, now found themselves priced out of the market; they started to employ charwomen as 'dailies' instead, and also to buy new labour-saving devices, such as vacuum cleaners, gas cookers and fires. At the same time, new publications like *The Ideal Servant-Saving House* by an Engineer and his Wife (1918) and *The Servant-less House* by R. Randal Phillips (1920) explained how householders could use this new technology to run their homes efficiently without servants.

For returning male servants, employment prospects were bleak. At the beginning of the war, *The Times* (12 August 1914) had urged the aristocracy to encourage their male staff to join up: 'There are large numbers of footmen, valets, butlers, gardeners, grooms, and gamekeepers, whose services are more or less superfluous and can either be dispensed with or replaced by women without seriously hurting or incommoding anybody.' This argument seems to have been in line with general opinion because in the early years of the twentieth century, male servants in private houses were increasingly seen as expensive luxuries. Parlourmaids were now taking on tasks previously undertaken by footmen and former butlers were being asked to work as single-handed men-servants. It did not help that the tax on male domestic servants, which had been in place since the late eighteenth century, was not repealed until 1937.

Male servants were now more often found working in hotels, clubs, restaurants and bars than in private households. After the war, previously wealthy landed estates had to cope with higher taxation, death duties and falling income from land, and the only way to balance the books was to reduce the numbers of their domestic staff. Just after the First World War, the family Eric Horne was working for as a butler cut its indoor staff from 25 to just three; his services were not retained. Afterwards, Eric worked as a single-handed butler for two years before looking for another place.

When he wrote his memoir, *What The Butler Winked At*, in 1923, Eric recalled:

> *I soon found there was a glut of unemployed butlers, and no places to be had ... and I found I had better have staid [sic] where I was. I advertised every week in the Morning Post, searched all the clubs in the West End of London and all places where butler's places are likely to be heard of, but to no effect.*

Excepting for a month's temporary work, I have had no employment for months. Everywhere it is parlourmaids, and married couples that are wanted. The married couples having to do the work of perhaps four servants that were kept previously.

More than half a million women were recorded as unemployed by March 1919, but the real figure would have been far higher as the official total did not include servants in private homes. Indoor domestic servants of both sexes (plus agricultural workers) were excluded from the new 1920 Unemployment Insurance Act, which provided the dole for manual workers, because they were not deemed to experience long periods of unemployment. If a woman had worked in domestic service before the war and tried to claim, then she could be reported and any benefit stopped because she did not qualify for the dole.

Although servants were not entitled to unemployment benefit, middle-class housewives, particularly readers of the popular press such as the *Daily Mail*, were convinced there were thousands of unemployed women who would rather scrounge on the dole than do decent work in domestic service. Some complained that the government should force the unemployed to work as maids when households such as their own were crying out for domestic help.

Indoor domestic servants remained outside the unemployment insurance legislation until 1948. Theirs was indeed a precarious existence. In her memoir, *Every Other Sunday*, Jean Rennie comments that after being dismissed from her first job in 1924, she was:

home, and unemployed ... I went on answering advertisements – for anything. I wrote countless letters; went to see managers of shops, works, offices. So many times I've done all that in the years. There was nothing. I did not, of course, get any unemployment benefit. Having been a domestic servant, you were not supposed to be out of a job, and anyway there was no Employment card, only the Health Insurance card. So, no benefit.

As a sop to middle-class employers, a clause was added to the National Insurance Act in 1921, requiring applicants to prove they were genuinely looking for work. If they were known to have refused a job as a servant, then their benefits could be withheld. However, the employers bemoaning the 'servant shortage' overlooked another factor: a high number of unemployed women had never worked in domestic service before and were completely unsuited for the work. Servants continued to be ridiculed in the national press as inept, so it is unsurprising that the public perception of them remained negative.

Two government reports were issued in the aftermath of the First World War to address the reluctance of women to return to domestic service. The first was the *Report of the Women's Advisory Committee on the Domestic Service Problem* (1919), carried out for the Ministry of Reconstruction. It came up with a number of recommendations, such as training schemes for girls to raise domestic service to a skilled occupation and compulsory written references, which 'should be restricted to definite statements, and should deal as little as possible with matters of opinion'. The reasons for women's reluctance to take up 'what should be recognised as an honourable profession' were identified as loss of social status by entering the occupation, long hours of duty and lack of companionship.

The sub-committee on organisation and conditions also stressed:

> 'We are convinced that much of the dissatisfaction and discomfort felt by workers and employers arises from preventable waste of labour and bad general conditions which could be remedied. Domestic workers will not take pleasure in their work as long as much of it consists in constantly carrying by hand for unnecessary distances, often up and down stairs, considerable weights of water, food and fuel, of tending heating and cooking apparatus undesirably wasteful of labour, and of the larger cleaning processes which could be better effected by outside workers furnished with mechanical appliances.

The problem was so complex that many of the Committee members felt unable to agree with the report's recommendations. Miss Lilian Harris disagreed with the Committee's main finding, that training was the most important question, stating: 'The objections of workers to domestic service are mainly due to the lack of freedom arising from living in the employer's house. This can only be met by a system of day workers living out, and paid an adequate wage.'

Jessie Stephen, with Alice Jarrett and Rosalind J. Whyatt, added a 'Memorandum on Wages' in which they put forward a recommended scale of weekly wages for various types of servant. They also suggested that:

> domestic workers should not be on duty more than eight hours per day exclusive of mealtimes and 'time off' ... We realise this is a revolutionary proposal but make it with the object of drawing the employers' attention to the necessity of so organising their households that maids will not, as at present, spend hours

on duty on the off-chance of visitors calling, or be employed in the cleaning of useless 'brights'. This we know to be one of the greatest grievances workers have.

These recommendations harked back to the main demands of the unions in the Edwardian period, which had never come to anything – nor did they this time.

In 1923, a second government report on domestic service was published, this time for the Minister of Labour, entitled the *Report of the Committee Appointed to Inquire into the Present Conditions as to the Supply of Female Domestic Servants.* A number of wide-ranging recommendations were made within the report, including the instruction of elementary school girls in domestic science between the ages of 12 and 14; advanced scholarships for girls desirous of completing specialised training; vocational courses for girls over the age of 14, together with grants where necessary, for individual pupils; and examinations with certificates to prove proficiency. It also suggested that registry offices should be controlled by local authorities, that unemployment benefit might be extended to cover all domestic servants and that employers and employees be represented on local committees 'to endeavour to agree upon conditions [of employment] in their area.'

Both reports highlighted the importance of social clubs for maids, particularly for single-handed young servants who had to cope with severe loneliness and could find companionship in the growing network of girls' clubs. The most popular ones were set up by the Young Women's Christian Association (YWCA) and the Girls' Friendly Society (GFS); by 1924, there were more than 350 registered GFS clubs across Britain. New to London and domestic service, Dolly Davey found a lifeline at her local YWCA branch, while Queenie Harris enjoyed regular dances at her GFS club.

The 1919 and 1923 reports produced similar findings but they failed to stem the exodus of young women and girls from domestic service, partly because the reports were simply shelved by the government and their recommendations were never acted upon.

Training for Servants

A young woman's aptitude for domestic service very often depended on the amount of training she had received in housework from her mother. By the twentieth century, this type of ad hoc training was not considered sufficient to provide quality candidates for servant vacancies. Training courses were created to fill the gap and local education authorities across the country ran domestic service schools for girls wishing to enter domestic service, as well as domestic economy schools for women who wanted to learn how to manage their own homes efficiently.

In 1914, there were just 10 domestic service training schools nationwide with provision for about 350 pupils. The number of girls being trained in these establishments by 1918 was only 220 and, although the reduced numbers was partly a result of the war, the 1919 report found 'there was amongst girls a growing distaste for domestic service under its present conditions, and a reluctance on the part of the parents to allow them to take up such work.'

There were 18 domestic economy schools in 1914, with a total provision for less than 700 pupils. Before the war, a fair proportion of the women had entered domestic service after completing their courses, yet the 1919 *Report* found that 'most of them are now taking up occupations in which the initial rate of payment is much higher'. The hundreds being trained in these schools were just a tiny fraction of those employed within the industry.

Practical but rudimentary domestic training was also provided in schools certified under the Poor Law Certified Schools Act (1862), and by charities such as the Girls' Friendly Society, the Metropolitan Association for Befriending Young Servants, the Church Army and the Salvation Army.

However, the domestic training most young girls received was provided in elementary schools as part of the curriculum from about the age of 12. A schoolgirl in the 1920s recalled her domestic science classes in Samuel Mullins and Gareth Griffiths' *Cap and Apron: An Oral History of Domestic Service in the Shires, 1880–1950*:

> *We did first of all cookery for about six months; we went one day a week to a cookery centre ... after that we went for six months to a laundry centre where we were taught laundry work. We had to take a garment from home each week; a woollen garment one week, cotton another, linen another, something embroidered another week ... then as we got to about thirteen years old we went to a 'home-making' centre and the teacher there lived in the house and we went every day for a month and we did everything in the house – cookery, laundry, shopping and housework, so that we got an overall picture of looking after a house.*

Hard Times

The 1920s and 1930s were an extremely difficult period in which to leave school and enter the workplace for the first time, given the high levels of unemployment during the worldwide economic depression. Bright working-class girls with grammar school scholarships whose fathers were out of work frequently had no choice but to enter domestic service. This generation were cheated of the opportunities education could offer them because of economic hard times.

One frequent barrier preventing the poorest young women from entering domestic service was the requirement to purchase their own uniform prior to starting work. The government addressed this issue by providing free uniforms to applicants who were willing to be employed as live-in domestic servants. A report from the Committee on Women's Training and Employment for 1923–24 stated that 3837 women had received this clothing, at a total cost of £12,470. If the servant remained in service for three months, then she was allowed to keep the outfit; if not, it had to be returned.

Training initiatives continued during the Depression era and in 1931, there were five residential, government-run training centres for domestic work administered by the Central Committee on Women's Training and Employment, at Newbold Beeches, Leamington Spa; Appleton Hall, Stockton Heath, Cheshire; The Elms, Market Harborough, Leicestershire; Harden, Long Benton, Newcastle-on-Tyne; and Millersneuk, Lenzie, Scotland.

Irene Thompson was born in Middlesbrough in 1918. She was one of the girls trained at The Elms in Market Harborough in around 1933 and she recalled her experiences in *Cap and Apron* by Samuel Mullins and Gareth Griffiths:

When I left school there were no jobs up there [in Redcar]. I took a little morning job at a boarding house. I used to work from eight until two for six shillings a week, scrubbing the front doorstep all morning. My mother was having a baby at the time and I stayed at home and looked after her, I was only just turned fourteen. A neighbour next door ... she was sending [her daughter] Grace to this training centre and she said would I like to go ... I had to go and pass one or two interviews and exams and things but they got me through and they sent me to Market Harborough ... It was a huge house and we done like a domestic science course, everything in three months, you was on the whole time, kitchen, bedroom work, cooking, needlework, knitting, even to making our own uniforms, blue dresses and starched aprons. They were a good crowd of girls, about 40, they were all about 14 to 17. We used to have a lot of fun. All you got was your keep; if you were under sixteen, you got a shilling a week, you went to the matron for that on a Friday. Sixpence was kept back so that when you left you had six shilling. If you were over sixteen you got 2s 6d a week and a shilling was kept back. They were very strict but we were happy. On the whole, I think

we were glad enough to get away from home and the poverty and everything.
They asked us what branch we wanted to go into ... These people who came,
they said they wanted a 'general' ... but I didn't mind because I'd always done
everything. I'd just been more or less polished off at the training centre.

One solution to the problem of mass unemployment was emigration to the Dominions, such as Canada and Australia. 'The Elms' had originally been opened in 1927 as a hostel established by the British and Australian governments to offer training facilities for women wanting to settle overseas. General servants were in particularly high demand in the former Dominions and government aid was provided in the form of training, along with assisted passages and guaranteed employment. After leaving school, Mollie Prendergast went into service but three of her siblings emigrated in the 1920s, splitting up the family forever.

The economic depression of 1929–1933 was most keenly felt in the old industrial areas, where communities relied on coal mining and shipbuilding for employment. In 1934, four 'Special Areas' of Britain were identified for specific government assistance to reduce the numbers of unemployed: South Wales, Tyneside, West Cumberland and industrial Scotland. Thousands of young men and women were sent to London and south-east England from the depressed 'Special Areas' to work in domestic service. David Dixon was sent to the capital from Cumbria on a YMCA scheme and was placed in service first as a houseboy, then as a cook.

Although women over 21 were granted the right to vote in 1928, this new independent status was not matched in the workplace. The mass unemployment of the 1920s meant that more working-class girls than ever were compelled to enter domestic service. In 1931, nearly one in five households had at least one live-in domestic servant. Around 1.3 million women were employed as indoor domestic servants at this time.

Domestic service continued throughout the 1930s and 1940s, largely because employing servants still represented respectability for the middle classes. They were the ultimate status symbol; if you could afford to keep a maid or two, then your neighbours and colleagues would know you were doing well. In *British Society 1914–45*, John Stevenson quotes a remark made by one middle-class woman in the early 1930s: 'I remember girls at school judging each other's wealth by the number of maids each had. And sometimes, I suspect, inventing an extra one to impress their friends. We had two.'

One way in which bright girls forced into domestic service could better themselves was to continue their education through evening classes. The Workers' Educational Association (WEA) was originally formed in 1903 for men, but it began to run evening classes for working women too, from 1905. However, servants had an additional obstacle to overcome to attend such classes, as they usually had to work in the evenings; an understanding employer was therefore required. Edith Hall attended WEA classes and gained qualifications which eventually enabled her to apply to train as a nurse, while Mollie Prendergast took advantage of similar opportunities during the Second World War.

Although the government appointed various committees to carry out investigations into the 'servant problem', nothing much was done, partly because other post-war issues were considered more important and worthy of funding. Perhaps most crucially, the fundamental issue of compelling employers to provide accurate characters was never enshrined in law. As Lucy Delap points out in her article, 'Yes, Ma'am: Domestic Workers and Employment Rights,' the fact that mistresses could withhold references or give a bad 'character' was 'key to keeping the balance of power on the side of employers, making servants reluctant to give any cause for complaint'.

The servant's place in society

Whether real or imagined, the stigma against servants still remained in the 1930s, a century after the footman William Tayler wrote about the issue in his diary. Mrs Selma Panter's story is told in *Cap and Apron* by Samuel Mullins and Gareth Griffiths. She was born in Gateshead on Tyneside in 1914 and, after leaving school at 14, worked in a sweet factory and then a bakery. At 15, she became a 'general' in a young household where the work was very hard. Her sister worked as a dormitory maid at Nevill Holt School, a preparatory school near Market Harborough, and through her, in 1932, Mrs Panter got a job at the school as a pantry maid, staying there for two years. She expressed her feelings about domestic service:

My mother didn't want me to go into service, because it was such a hard life. You were at their beck and call, they owned you, really owned you. Service was actually looked down on you know. I remember going into my mother-in-law's, after I was married and there was a woman there and she said, "Oh, a maid," and her nose went tip high. And I said, "Yes, my word, I really worked for my money." You know I was really looked down on. And there was no social

*security then and no dole for servants. Once you had left your job you were on
your own.*

Similar sentiments appeared within the testimony of a parlourmaid on attitudes
to servants, which was included in the 1923 government report:

*I do not believe any girl minds the work. They do mind being ridiculed. I have
suffered untold misery by the name 'only a servant'. Invitations out state "Be
sure and do not let it be known you are a domestic. We should not like our friends
to mix with servants." It is the snobbery of our own class.*

A new dimension was added to the 'servant problem' from 1935, when
increasing numbers of foreign workers arrived in Britain on Ministry of Labour
domestic permits, particularly Jewish refugees from Germany and Austria. In
1938, 13,792 such permits were issued. From 1938, the Domestic Bureau of
the Central Committee for Refugees was charged with securing Home Office
permits for refugee domestics. The problem was that many of the applicants
were middle-class, probably having employed maids themselves back home, and
were often completely unsuited to the work. Although many stayed in domestic
service, others moved into alternative jobs when they became available.

During the Second World War, the rearmament programme once more
provided women with the opportunity of well-paid factory work. For those who
remained in service, a new problem arose: thousands of families from London
and other large cities were evacuated to the countryside, leaving their servants
behind and putting them out of work. The fact they were still not entitled to
unemployment benefit made the situation extremely difficult.

In 1945, another government report was commissioned: *Post-War Organisation
of Private Domestic Employment* by Violet Markham and Florence Hancock.
Markham and Hancock described domestic service as 'the oldest, the largest
and the most unorganised form of women's employment ... A thoughtless
mistress with a touch of the tyrant in her composition can make life a perpetual
fret for her staff. Or by tact and consideration she may make its burden almost
inappreciable.' Unsurprisingly, the report made similar recommendations to
those of 1919 and 1923: to regulate the industry, provide good wages and legally
require employers to meet minimum standards for working conditions.

In *My Ancestor Was in Service*, Pamela Horn quotes Mildred White, a
correspondent to Violet Markham who was a cook-housekeeper in Cheltenham.
By 1945, she had worked for her employer for 16 years:

We both know that I could get three times the wage she is able to pay but I have not met anyone else that I would work for in this capacity. I see so many who are so selfish, who treat their maids as machines, give them little or no comforts, and certainly no respect ... We have always shown the greatest respect for each other ... I am so very, very happy in my work.

As a domestic servant who was demonstrably valued by her employer, Mildred White was a dying breed. By 1951, there were just 724,000 female indoor domestic servants recorded on the census. It was no coincidence that, for the first time, clerks and typists constituted the largest occupation for women with 1,271,000 employed. The desire for independence, a convivial working atmosphere and fixed hours had won out; domestic service would never again be seen as the natural occupation for girls and women.

Mollie Prendergast

Between-maid and Housemaid

Born in 1907 in Hallthwaites, Millom in Cumbria, Mollie Prendergast (née Shaw) had three older sisters and a brother, as well as two younger sisters. Her father was a quarryman and the family moved to Rose Cottage, Broughton-in-Furness, Cumbria in 1912. Mollie went into domestic service when she left school. She met her first husband while in service and married in 1928.

This extract is taken from her unpublished memoir, *Memoirs of Mollie Prendergast* from LSE Library's Collections (Ref. 7MOP) and is reproduced with their kind permission.

In November 1920, when I was 13, I was allowed to leave school, a year earlier than the leaving age of fourteen because I had never missed attendance. By this time Mabel and Evelyn, my older sisters had been working away in domestic service some years. There were four girls and one brother at home, but Annie, who had stayed home to help Mother with the young ones, went off to service and my time came before my fourteenth birthday. I didn't mind because it was helping our parents. There was so much unemployment that domestic service was the only way we could earn some money, get housed and fed.

The two younger members, Elsie and Marjorie were the exception and I was very glad that they didn't have to go into domestic service. Education at the local school had improved. The teachers we had, Mr and Mrs Parkinson, retired on the day I left school and the new teacher was very enthusiastic to get more children through scholarships. We had never been told about them; only the schoolteachers', bank managers' and professionals' children were told about the scholarships to the Grammar School. They were called George Moore Scholarships, after a benefactor who set up a fund to help working class children get an education ... I did regret that I missed a good education. I'm sure the teachers did their best but to leave school at 13, what could I expect.

Ambleside is only nine miles from Coniston but it was difficult to get to. I took the train to Coniston and then went by horse and coach up the steep hills. Sometimes we had to get out and push because the horses couldn't cope. The advertisement said, "Must be Church of England and have no followers." Fancy, I was only 13.

My employers were two very religious ladies, Miss Bowers and her niece Miss Boland. They had a cook, a house parlour maid and me. I was a between maid and if there is anything a "tweenie" is not expected to do, I never found it. I became quite the expert at plucking and drawing chickens, pheasants, partridges and rabbits. I didn't like it as I rather loved rabbits, but had no choice: sentiment wasn't allowed.

I wore print dresses made by Mother in the morning and a white hat and apron. Mother also made the black afternoon dress. The afternoon cap had two long tails. The employer provided the aprons and caps. I was very upset that my employer didn't like my print dresses because they didn't have enough tucks in the back. When the dressmaker came in they wanted her to add some material, but she wouldn't because she said they were made nicely.

The two ladies who employed me were very religious and we had to go to church several times a week and it was quite a long way up very steep hills. The nephew and brother was the local vicar. We had to attend prayers every night and I was so tired I often went to sleep. I fell off the seat several times and they decided it was a waste of time. I was not alone as Miss Bowers, who was behind a screen, used to snore during prayers.

Young people used to come to the house to study preparation for Confirmation and the employer asked if I would join. In fact, she wrote to Mother to ask her permission and Mother in her wise way said that I should decide myself and would agree to whatever I said. I thought about it and because I felt that I did not wish to join the employer who was not a really good person, I said no. I don't think she liked me much after that.

At 13, in some ways I was very grown up. I could make bread and jam, but I was also very naïve. Even though Mother was very intelligent, she hadn't talked to me about sex and I didn't know anything about it. We didn't even learn anything about sex from the animals and when the billy goat came to the goats, it was all very hush hush!

Millicent, aged 21, who was the cook, came from Millom. We shared a room and she was very kind to me and told me some of the things I didn't know. She was engaged to be married and her young man who was unemployed, cycled over to see her every second Sunday.

I was very homesick especially at night. I particularly missed the younger ones, which included Tommy and Marjorie Smart who were living at Rose Cottage.

My sisters Elsie and Marjorie wrote to me. The work I did as a domestic servant was not helpful in gaining an education as we got very little free time and were not expected to take any interest in what went on in the outside world. We never seemed to see newspapers and of course there wasn't radio or TV.

I was fortunate that I had relations down in Ambleside. I say down, because the house was on a steep turning off a steep climb called Kirkstone Pass, a lonely place with a waterfall nearby, the sound of which made it seem even lonelier. I could visit relations one half-day a week or half-day every other Sunday. I was lucky one of the relations, Jack Shuttleworth, a cousin of mother's, had three daughters.

The other family was great-uncle John Shuttleworth's. They were all adults but very kind and one of the boys would walk back to the house with me when it got dark. I was always nervous of the dark, especially outside. I don't know why as I had no reason to be afraid. I did appreciate the kindness of the two families.

There was very little transport in the winter and when I went home at Christmas, I went by steamer from Ambleside to the other end of Lake Windermere to Lakeside then by train to Ulverston and then another train to Foxfield, two miles from Broughton. When I went to get on the train, the man gave me a half-price ticket and I didn't tell him I was over 13. When I went back I walked the nine miles from Coniston to Ambleside as there were no coaches in winter. When I was young it did not seem very difficult and we were used to walking after all.

I was shocked at the way Millicent was treated when she was taken ill with influenza. She worked too long before the doctor was sent for and when she came back from the doctor, she leant on the dresser because she was so weak and was told to get away from there. She was sent home to Millom, a town very badly hit by the "slump" as it was called. When she went, I went too as I was leaving because Mother thought I had had enough. After [Millicent's] holiday I went to see her at Foxfield on her way back to Ambleside. She looked very ill and contracted TB and later died. I still have a long letter she wrote telling me of the treatment she received when she returned. How could I ever forgive them!

I left the place in Ambleside at the time our brother Bill went to Australia. Things were getting worse and young people were encouraged to emigrate to the Empire. When our brother finished his apprenticeship as an engineer, he took any work he could get, working for local farmers or making roads. After some time, our parents and brother Bill agreed that he would go to Australia having a sister there able to nominate him [the oldest sister, Mabel, had emigrated after the First World War when she married an Australian serviceman]. Our parents were very sad, especially mother and it was the first time that I saw [her] cry.

Cheap emigration took thousands of young men and women to the Empire. Thousands and thousands went in ships and many were the best of British youth. Many had trades, some got before the war and others like our brother had just finished his apprenticeship at Barrow Shipyards and couldn't find work in his trade.

Later in 1928, two other sisters, Annie and Elsie, went to Australia. Annie, who had been in domestic service in London, had managed to train, through evening classes, as a hairdresser. Elsie had trained as a shorthand typist.

Our two young sisters, Elsie and Marjorie, had a better opportunity to learn and went on to Grammar School and Commercial College. I was pleased for them and so was mother, who was a believer in education and still had quite a struggle buying books, uniforms and so on. Father still worked hard for low wages ...

It was time I left Ambleside because I was feeling very tired and was happy to relax more when I got home. I returned to [a] love of reading and conversation. We had newspapers and magazines. Our parents discussed current affairs a lot and were interested in those who were advocating better living standards.

Although Mother had only a limited education, she read and thought a lot about local and world events. In those days there was no National Health Service, but there was a district nurse and a committee dealing with organising this, collecting money and putting on events, such as whist drives, dances and jumble sales. Mother took part in all this ... I remember Mother also telling us about the Suffragettes and what they had to do to get women the vote. I was 21 in 1928 and in 1929 there was an election and women could vote at 21 for the first time.

I stayed at home some months then went to a situation in Norton, Yorkshire. An older sister, Evelyn was working as cook housekeeper at a very large house at Malton, a few miles away, so in fact got me the place as second housemaid, which meant better training and a much bigger staff.

Colonel and Mrs Brewis (she had the money) had a young family, three girls and a boy. There were two governesses, one nanny, two housemaids, two parlour maids, three kitchen staff and the outdoor staff. Evelyn and I used to visit one another. She rode a bike. I had a boyfriend, a groom, aged 15, a very nice boy. I had happy times there. We used to go to dances.

I was there for two years, then Mrs Behrens (she was a Rothschild) wanted a second housemaid in London and I was proposed. Evelyn remained in Yorkshire and married Harold Horner and had two daughters … They all eventually moved to Australia.

I moved to London to 34 Princess Gate, which was just used for the London Season, but I was there all the time, part of a skeleton staff of three kitchen, one butler, two parlour maids, one hall boy, one head housemaid and a daily. Lil Happy was the head housemaid and she often took me to her home. They were the only outsiders I met. Don't think we had a lazy life!

We had a burglary and Lil said we needed protection [*they got a watchdog*]. Of course he had no idea. I used to take him to Hyde Park [for walks]. Ann (Annie) my older sister was also working in London for the Dowager Duchess of Westminster and later for a Greek tycoon.

Miss Peggy Behrens married Peter Harris and they lived in the house. That's how I met Bill Packham, who was a chauffeur/valet to Peter Harris. Bill had been batman to Peter Harris, an Officer in the Coldstream Guards during the First World War and after the war he contacted Bill and asked him to be his chauffeur/valet.

Then I worked temporarily for Mrs Sturgess, George Meredith's daughter and then permanently for the Joels, who lived in Grosvenor Square. But there were too many people on the staff and I didn't have enough to do and I didn't know many of them, so I went back to the Sturgess'.

When the 1926 strike was on, the rich did everything to break the strike [but] I didn't know much about politics then. I developed a housemaid's knee (not a prayer knee; there was no danger of that) and had an operation in the Ulverston Hospital between 1926 and 1927.

On August 4th 1928, I married Wesley Packham (known as Bill) in Broughton, just before Ann and Elsie went to Australia. I stopped work and I was very lonely. Bill had to go to work, night after night. When the Harris' heard I was lonely, "to keep Mollie happy" they got me a little dog, named Terry, from their country place.

During the Second World War, Mollie joined the Communist Party and was involved in ARP work. She took advantage of free evening and day classes to improve her education. Her husband died in 1951 and afterwards, she joined the Civil Service and became a political activist for health and housing. Mollie remarried in 1958 to Jim Prendergast and was widowed again in 1974. She retired in 1977.

Edith Hall

General Servant

Edith Hall (née Acreman) was born in 1908 in a small town on the Uxbridge Road, near Hayes, Middlesex. On leaving school in 1922, she alternated between a string of factory jobs and working in domestic service. She also attended a Workers' Educational Association evening class, which later enabled her to train as a nurse.

This extract is taken from Edith's memoir, *Canary Girls and Stockpots* (1977), which was written as a result of a project with the Luton Workers' Educational Association. It is reproduced with the kind permission of the Workers' Educational Association.

L eaving school at fourteen had a traumatic effect on me. I longed to learn more but this proved to be very difficult after working fifty hours a week and then having to help at home. After working from early morning until at least six at night, I attended the local grammar school for what were then called 'night schools'. There were very few subjects on the curriculum besides reading, writing and arithmetic ... After a few months I was told to take two shillings and sixpence to enable me to sit an R.S.A. exam in English, which the teacher seemed to think I might pass. We just did not have the money to spare.

My first job was at an electric lamp works, where I was obliged to walk over a mile each way. I was so small that the time-keeper thought I had brought my father's dinner and that I was not seeking employment ...

I left the factory for a short break and went into service when I was fifteen. Mother would have preferred me to be placed in 'good service' as she had been in her time, but I went as a 'maid of all work'. I was expected to wait at table, getting my own meals when I could, there being no allotted times for the servant. I took the food into the dining-room and was given a plate with mine served ready to eat, which I would take back into the kitchen and eat standing up by the draining board, or at least attempt to, because by the time I had taken the vegetables round to the other diners at the table and returned, mine was invariably cold. There was no point in my sitting down because in about ten or twelve minutes the bell would ring for the sweet to be brought in. Before I could start on my sweet, the bell would ring again for me to clear the table.

These conditions were the norm for a general servant or 'generals' as we were called. Many of my school friends became 'skivvies' by the fact of being females and there being very little other work for them, other than in one of the factories. It used to amuse me when factory girls looked down on us as inferior, calling us 'drain 'ole cleaners'. Some maids, after a long period in service, acquired the accents of their employers and, in their turn, looked down on factory girls and thought them 'common'.

A 'general' was expected to do all the housework, preparing the vegetables and the cooking. I had to be up at six-thirty in the morning and clean the master's shoes and get the children's clothes ready for school. I was small for fifteen and their own daughter, who was thirteen, had reached pubescence and I had not; I was never treated as a child in any way, or even as a young person.

When my master or mistress went out at night, I was expected to stay up in case one of the young children woke and called. I was left plenty of ironing to do and silver to clean just in case I got sleepy; then up again next morning early.

There was little personal time at all but I used to steal a few minutes very late at night peeping into the master's books. His wife said she couldn't understand them so she was sure I could not either. I was only allowed to dust them when she was there. My memories of that place are that I was always tired, always hungry and listening to the wrangling of my employers.

I was told that I smelled which, if true, would not have been surprising as I was not allowed to use the bathroom; I would not have had time anyway. He was a sub-editor on one of the London newspapers, and years later, when reading his obituary, I saw that it ended with 'He had a wonderfully happy marriage'. Not whilst I was there, he didn't. I wonder why the Marriage Guidance Council don't employ servants or charladies who have really seen it all from the inside?

When I was sixteen I took a daily part-time post as I was needed at home in the afternoons. It seemed to mother that I was being starved as part-timers weren't fed, except this one occasion. It was Christmas time and the lady for whom I worked had persuaded me to stay for midday dinner, although I had persisted in telling her my own family would not start Christmas dinner without me. I must have been naïve if I thought that she meant me to sit at the table with the family, there was no room on the kitchen table where all the food was laid out so I had mine on the draining board (again) by the sink. I was full of self-pity thinking, 'Here I am, sitting by the sink, having my Christmas dinner, while they're all waiting for me at home'. She had kept me there, the cunning thing, knowing that no servant would have a meal and then walk out leaving the washing-up and kitchen untidy. When I reached home in mid-afternoon the family had had their dinner, except mother who would not have hers until I was home. I didn't get a penny extra for that afternoon's work; but, after all, I had been given my meal.

So back to another factory, this time to 'His Master's Voice', now 'E.M.I.'. I was employed on a machine for drilling metal discs, a day's work being a full truck-load ... Although there was mass unemployment, I had been adept at finding work for the first three years after leaving school; this, no doubt, was due to the low rate of pay that young women received. After this period, employment became much more difficult to find. I must have had seventeen jobs by this time I was seventeen, leaving each, as I thought to better myself ... but I never did. Changing one unskilled job for another is rather like exchanging council houses; one is very much like the one just left.

On one occasion, I did manage to get a job as a shop assistant and when the boss appeared to be asking my opinion on an aspect of the work, I started to say, "Well, I think ..."; he interrupted me with, "I do the thinking here, you're paid to do the work." It was a pity I had to leave, I rather liked the thought of being a sales lady.

The adverts for a maid-of-all-work used to read, 'Young girl wanted to train as domestic', but I soon realised that I was a little more intelligent than were some of my mistresses. There was one lady who insisted that I call her '*Ma*dam' and was not at all pleased when I persisted in saying 'M'*dam*' which I thought gave more emphasis to her supposed status. She made me scrub her kitchen with strong soda water which took the pattern off her lino and the skin off my hands. Even a most exhausting polishing couldn't restore the sheen. When I suggested just a soapy wash instead of the scrubbing away of the lovely floral pattern, she admonished me with, "Now, Edith, you're getting lazy." Then she would start to talk to me in confidence and tell me her troubles, young as I was, but when I started to mention my own affairs she responded with, "There you go, Edith, you're chattering away again; now, get on."

She confided to me once that she and her husband 'didn't bother with that'; I didn't tell her that I had seen a packed of naked lady pictures in a little cupboard by his bed. She would tell me to use their old underclothes as dusters but as she would not have me wash them first before use, I found the smell of Madam, Master and polish somewhat overpowering. Furthermore, I was always hungry there. When I told her that I was leaving to better myself she said, "Well, don't ask me for a reference, you have a good post here." So I wrote out a good one myself and gave a friend's name who was in service in a big house, and she sent it off for me to the next place. No-one ever discovered that she was the maid and not the mistress. After that, some of my in service friends used to ask me for references when their employers would not give one if they considered the maid had left for no valid reason.

It must have been very lonely for a young girl, coming from her own large family, to be placed in a one-servant household. Being a gregarious young woman, I obtained a position in a large house where there were other maids. Here, I was called by my surname as Acreman, my maiden name, was unusual and distinctive, but few seemed able to pronounce it correctly. One young orphan girl from a well-known children's home, who came to us was happy to be in a large house but she stayed only a few weeks because her name was the same as one of the daughters of the house; to overcome the difficulty the master said to her, "I will call you Abigail; it is from the Bible and means serving maid." He was a deeply religious man and so everything should have worked out all right; but the new Abigail had difficulty in recognising herself when called and appeared disobedient. Not knowing who were her parents, the bewildered young girl would say, "Who am I? I don't think I'm Abigail; I wonder who I am."

The elderly father of the master was an invalid and had his own resident male attendant who slept in his room. This man was not a bit grateful for his post in view of the fact of so many other men being out of work. He ranted on to us each evening about having a wife and child and that he should be going home to them each night. He was allowed home one weekend a month and an afternoon each week. Apparently the old gentleman couldn't be trusted with a female nurse; he had had one but had bought her expensive presents.

There was also a little poodle dog upstairs who received a great deal of attention; we sometimes had the animal's dinner sent back because it was said to be too thin; the gravy, they said, was not rich enough. As we were not given anything to thicken the gravy, we kept a candle with which to stir it until it did look rich and nourishing. Everything was such a rush, we hardly had an alternative ...

I must still have been flitting from one job to another because in my lunch hour at one factory, I went out and was taken on at a sweet factory, where I started next morning. These sweet factories all had the same type of enrobing machines. These machines covered creams and toffees with chocolate and it was a very boring job to keep the travelling belt always filled with the centres. We were allowed eight minutes break for refreshments and we used to take Oxo cubes to make a hot drink. But my young fellow-worker Molly and myself broke the monotony by putting our meat cubes on the enrobing machine and getting them covered in chocolate. We thought it funny, imagining the 'tart' and her 'feller' in the 'pictures' biting into the meat cube covered in chocolate. Molly and I used to be on that machine ten hours a day sometimes ...

The depression was certainly deepening now because the next job I went after turned out to be a step backwards. The time-keeper I went to said that the only thing he could offer me was to take the tea-trolley round until things brightened up again, then I could go into the factory. This I reluctantly accepted ...

Trying to catch up on one's education after a long day at work was very difficult and I well understood my father's problems as he had left school at the age of twelve to start work. Every evening he would pore over *Harmsworth's Encyclopaedia* and a self-educator and together we went to a class organised by the Worker's Educational Association. I had some difficulty in that when I was a skivvy in a one-servant household, there would be the washing-up to do when I returned from my night class on my evening off which meant changing back into my maid's clothes and washing up the dirty dishes left from the supper I had prepared before leaving for the class.

But now, with what joy, tired out physically but mentally alert did my dear dad and I discuss our class together over supper which mother had prepared for us, *and* she would additionally help us by washing up afterwards ...

When I was nineteen years old, I thought I was educationally fit enough to apply for training as a nurse. After several months of letter writing to hospitals I realised that there was little chance of my becoming a probationer if I kept revealing that I had been a factory girl and a housemaid so the next application form I received I just filled in the bare essentials and ignored the more pertinent questions but enclosed a glowing reference from my evening school teacher as to my character and giving no information as to any previous employment except to say that my parents didn't believe in young women going out to work with the exception of nursing; something of an exaggeration because I must have had about twenty jobs by then. With this white lie I obtained the first post I then applied for.

Queenie Harris

Between-maid and Parlourmaid

Born in 1909 in Wycombe End, Beaconsfield, Queenie Harris (née Leslie) was the eldest of five children and the only daughter. Her father was a gardener for Lord Burnham and Queenie went into service in 1923. This extract is taken from her unpublished memoir, which she wrote for her family and it is reproduced with the kind permission of her daughter-in-law, Pam Harris.

At fourteen my school days came to an end and sad I was at leaving them behind me, for I loved my school days. They were so happy and free. There was not much to offer for us girls at that time, only going into service, and being the eldest and only girl, my mother did not wish to part with me altogether, so I went out daily.

My first job was in the house of Mr and Mrs Tidy, helping generally with the housework. I stayed there for eight months until my mother was taken ill with a broken ulcer on her ankle so she had to take to her bed. At 15½, I was little mother to my four brothers and my father. I cooked and cleaned the cottage, nursed my mother, while my two aunts did the washing and ironing between them. It took my mother two months to get on her feet, but we all rallied round, supervised by my grandmother, my mother's mother.

My cousins and I were more like sisters and my cousin being a year older than me suggested we worked together if a situation arose and strangely enough it did. So at sixteen and Nen (short for Nellie) at seventeen, we were both interviewed for the posts of housemaid and between-maid for a widow and housekeeper. There was also a cook and butler. Now this was a very large house called 'Harrias' and the last occupier was the Hon. Miss Lake, daughter of Lord and Lady Burnham of that time.

It was a lovely house comprising of six bedrooms, dressing-rooms and three bathrooms, also a boudoir. Each one of the staff had their own bedroom and downstairs was a large drawing- and dining-room and housekeeper's room. There were also servants' quarters comprising of butler's pantry, servants' hall and kitchens and garden. It was an easy to run house as it was so beautifully furnished. Blue was the colour of the Lady's bedroom, autumn colours of the housekeeper's room and on the other side of the corridor was a real man's room kept specially for her nephew, who would arrive any time of an evening for dinner in his light aeroplane, landing in the field next to the house! We had many staying visitors at this lovely house and the lady of the house entertained very lavishly. It was hard work but we enjoyed every minute of it. We were a happy foursome, joined by a helper for the rough work.

After 18 months, our first butler and cook left for a better situation so we had to get used to another couple. They were very good, the wife an excellent cook, but oh dear, the husband had bouts of liver complaints, so he said, and more often than not would be found fast asleep when he should be attending to lunch or dinner. The last straw came when we were having an important luncheon party. My cousin who had covered up before could not this time as instead of butler and housemaid waiting at table it was housemaid and between-maid with housekeeper hovering in the backroom and daily helper doing my job in the kitchen. After all was done and washed up he woke up, for even his wife could not wake him before. You can guess what happened – 24 hours' notice for them. We were so sorry for his wife.

My cousin and I, with the help of the housekeeper and daily helper, ran the house as the lady had decided to move. She did not like stopping in one place for too long. We had very happy memories of our days there although we worked hard. We laughed a lot and had our free time off. With my other two older cousins, we joined our Girls' Club and always went to London on a day off once a month to the theatre. After various owners (one was Lord Reith of the BBC), the house later became a home for paying guests who did not wish to live on their own and what lovely surroundings they had to come to in the twilight of their days.

From there I worked temporarily at two jobs and then settled in nicely at Hall Barn Cottage as parlour maid, which I very much enjoyed owing to the wonderful tuition of my cousin Nen as we had gone our separate ways by then. The people I worked for had come from the husband's job in India so you can imagine what lovely plate silver and glass I had to work with. It was such a joy to lay the table. They entertained lavishly and the conversation was most varied as at these dinner parties I never left the dining-room. We had tea parties too when nothing but French was spoken. It was most intriguing as I could not understand a word.

It was a very friendly atmosphere working in this house and we were more or less treated as equals, not mistress and maid. After I had been there about two years the master of the house became ill and rather crotchety, so me being the quietest I found I was doing the housemaid's work as well as my own. I was told to do the early morning tea call and as Beaconsfield Church struck 7am, I had to knock on the door with it. The whole of the time I was there I was never late, which meant of course my day started at 6.30am. Also the stairs from the top of the house, did I mention it? It was a three storey house, so you might guess that no-one objected to this arrangement.

In the summer time we had tennis parties at weekends, and lemonade and punch had to be taken up to the tennis courts which were a good ¾ mile through the gardens. But with all that to do we were a very happy family all told and of course, we had our free time, one half day a week, either half day Saturday or Sunday and often an hour off if we asked other days. The pay I was getting in them days was no more than 15 shillings per week and our food. We had the same as the dining room which was not always the thing in those days and of course, a few shillings went a long way in those days.

There were no buses in Beaconsfield then, so we had to walk. There were trains to Wycombe and London but outlying distances we either had to walk or cycle. So you might not think it much, but we managed. A bar of chocolate would be 2d, sweets 2d a quarter, and the pictures 1/- up to 2/6. Then there were the dances we would go to, our 6d hops as we called them and we thoroughly enjoyed ourselves. The dances would be from 7.30pm until 10 or 10.30pm if we asked for extra time. Our Girls' Club was run by our old school teacher Miss Cordelia Wright. We paid 6d a week for this. We were taught to dance here so we could enjoy other dances when we went. Also, we rehearsed and performed many plays, and twice a year a grand social was given. One of my cousins was very versatile and people would come for miles to hear her monologues of the poor servant girls she used to portray. Also in all the sketches, we others used to give a song and dance routine and dance in between, all for the grand price of 1/-.

What fun we all had for we always had a new dress for the occasion and the excitement when we got back on who was there and who we danced with! I was the youngest of our little party and very much teased by my cousins, which I took in good part for at one 6d hop, I was asked after a dance by a young man a bit older than me. From then on, I was never without a partner as he always turned up at every dance, which was a great pastime for us girls in those days. But that was all he was, a dancing partner, for I met my husband off the dance floor as he did not dance.

After two and a half years of happy harmony working with the cook and housemaid, who by the way were sisters, they left and things were never the same. A local girl came first as housemaid who I knew and we worked well together. But the cook was new to us and in an establishment of three, the cook usually rules the roost. She made no difference to me as I was quite confident in my job and I had my own pantry where I was always kept very busy keeping the silver up to perfection, but alas not the housemaid. Often there were clashes of temper. Our food was part of our wages and we had noticed cutting down on food, especially at breakfast time and had mentioned the matter to the cook who promptly denied it. But one morning it came to a head.

The housemaid had finished her early morning duties and was in the kitchen when our breakfast was being cooked. She saw bacon cut up, two slices between three of us and two eggs scrambled between three. All fury broke out as the cook could not deny it this time. Raised voices brought the mistress and myself from the dining room where I was serving their meal and wanting to know what the trouble was about. She saw for herself and said to me: "Has it happened before?" and of course, I had to say, "Yes." You might guess how popular we each were after that and thought the cook would leave after a right telling off, but she did not. But the housemaid did, as she said to me: "I'm not stopping here. It will never be the same again."

But I stopped as the cook knew she had to work with me, I being parlour-maid and no more nonsense and I was nearer her age. So strangely enough, my younger cousin came to work under me just as I had worked and been trained by her older sister so all was harmony once more, and no more cutting down of food. Hall Barn Cottage was my second home in those days as my family with my parents still lived in Windsor End and I saw them often.

During the first three years I was there, the wine which was drunk at mealtimes was discussed with me as, of course, I wanted to know what glasses to use. From then, I was given the key to the cellar and told what to get and open it and sample it to see if it was alright. Although, don't think I ever acquired the taste for wine – I did not! I thought some of it was horrid. During my stay there, I met my husband and I'm afraid we were not allowed any male friends in. For a time it did not bother us as we were only friends going for walks or to the pictures and he played football for Wooburn Green. My four brothers played for Beaconsfield, so that was another thing I had to get interested in and go and watch.

As time went by and we decided to get married, he thought once a week was not much time for seeing anyone. So after five years, and they were happy years,

I went daily, but I did not like it. I missed the company, I missed all the treasures I had been used to, but most of all I missed the polished table, the gleaming silver and glass I had laid for my last dinner party. I was not there long as a daily when a cottage was offered to us through my future father-in-law and we got married in September 1931.

Queenie got married in 1931 and had two children. She died in 2003.

Cissie Ewen

Housemaid

Elizabeth (Cissie) Ewen (née Cave) was born in 1912 in Percy Main, Northumberland. She was one of 11 children, two of whom died in early childhood. Her father, a coal miner, died when Cissie was just six years old. Before she married, Cissie's mother had worked as a kitchen-maid at a large hall in County Durham.

Having left school at the age of 14, Cissie worked first for the owner of a market garden. In her second year there, the owner got married and she was given a full-time job in the house.

This extract about her time in domestic service is taken from her unpublished memoirs, originally written for her family, and is reproduced with the kind permission of her children, John Ewen, Kathleen McNeill and Anne Newton.

The following year [my employers] had twins, so from then on I was never sure what time I was going to finish, for I had to help with the babies as well as the work, help feed them and take them out and often stay until they were settled for the night.

When they were about six or seven months old, I was laid up with a sprained ankle, so for about three weeks I couldn't go to work and she had to get the help of another girl. When I was ready to go back, she said to me, "You're never going to better yourself here: why not try for something else where you may better yourself?"

I then got a job in Kirton Gardens, about 20 minutes' walk from home working for a Mrs Wood. Their married daughter, husband and child lived with them: their name was Bradbury. Bobby, their three-year-old boy was just beautiful and very bright. Mrs Bradbury was about my height, maybe a little bigger made, and very nice and easy to get on with.

I was with them about two years before they moved away to live in Wallsend. While with them, Mrs Bradbury gave me the opportunity of having the clothes she was finished with, instead of letting them go to a second-hand clothes dealer who came calling every so often to see if she had any to sell and gave her very little for a bagful. She never asked very much for them from me and our Maggie and I got some lovely dresses and always felt well-dressed after that.

I remember while working there one day, Bobby noticed I was wearing a nice collar on my dress and he said, "You have Mammy's collar on – take it off." At that moment, his mother came on the scene and explained to him it was no longer hers, she had given it to me.

I also remember another time while there and I was wearing a lovely long-sleeved blouse I'd got from her. It was a fine, soft sort of material, and while busy at the gas stove adjusting the pots over the gas rings, I reached over the front one (which I had on high) to see to the pot on the back ring. The flame ran right up my arm to my shoulder and down again and the sleeve didn't burn, nor turn black, nor even smell of smoke. It looked just the same, but I got a big fright. There was no-one else in the house, and I had been in a hurry to get the dinner started.

There was another time when I was alone in the house. It was a big two-storey one, and I heard a voice saying, "There's someone at the door." I thought I'd imagined it, but I still went to look; there was no one there. The same thing happened a second time. I began to feel nervous on my way to the back of the house where I'd been busy. I passed through the kitchen and heard it again and found it came from a relative's parrot that they were taking care of. They hadn't mentioned it could talk! After that, I heard it saying quite a few sentences.

Once they moved to Wallsend, and I found it was too far and too expensive to travel each day, I started looking for another job. It was then that I started working at the Tynemouth Infirmary less than 10 minutes' walk from Silkey's Lane, though I lived in. My job was corridor maid and I had to look after the nurses' quarters in the new buildings, and once or twice a week clean out the maids' rooms in the old buildings. The rooms were really old; they were attics with their windows high up on the roof.

My wages were £1 19 shillings 2 pence one month and £1 19 shillings 10 pence the next: the difference was something to do with the stamps on my card for insurance [National Insurance], I'm not sure now. I gave Mam the pound and I kept the rest to clothe myself and other expenses. It meant saving a long while to get anything like a coat. Fortunately, small things and shoes weren't expensive.

I had two evenings and a half-day a week off. I had to take over the doctors' and matron's maid's duty when she was off duty and two nights a week, I had to take over the telephone job because the office girl worked only a nine to five, five days a week job. After I had been there for a few months, the doctors' and matron's maid left and I was put into her position. There were two doctors, sometimes three and they seemed to stay only for a few months then move on. I think they came straight from medical school to the Infirmary; then, from there they tried to get into partnership in a private practice.

While the job wasn't as heavy work as corridor maid, I often had to hang around in the evenings, waiting until the matron returned after she'd been out, just to take her up a glass of hot milk. I suppose if I'd complained about it, I might have been able to get one of the night nurses to take it up.

After working at the hospital for about two years, I fancied a change and wrote after a job in a private house in Alona Place. They were very big three-storey houses on one side of the street, and ordinary ones on the other. I got the job in this big house, which had a very long path from the gate or street entrance to the front door. When I told the girls at the hospital where I was going to work, one of them said, "You'll never stay. I've been there and they're terrible." One of the nurses had an aunt living opposite, who told her that they changed their maids every week; no one would work for them. I soon found out why they couldn't get anyone to stay.

They were real slave drivers. There was a widow and two daughters, the eldest one was very nice but away from home all day working. The mother, and younger daughter who was engaged to a doctor, were the ones I had dealings with. They were wealthy fishing boat owners and as mean as sin. I had to use six sticks and one match to light the fires in the mornings; after that, I had to light the gas ring from paper spills I had made in the evenings. The mats in the kitchen were taken up in the mornings, even in winter, so I spent most of my time with a cold bare floor. They were put down again shortly before I went to bed, for I had to wait till I was all finished which was near bedtime, before being allowed to put them down.

The other people in the big houses employed men to clear the snow away from their paths to the street entrances; I had to do ours. The old lady said I was to call her Madam, and she said they couldn't afford to give me bacon and egg each morning as they had, but I could have it once a week. I had to wear two different uniforms: morning and change for afternoon and evening which took my wages for the time I stopped there; then I had to get one shilling and sixpence from Mam to make up the difference. I worked a week then put in a week's notice. They were really mad that I left.

John [Cissie's fiancé] was waiting out the front to carry my case, but the Madam got annoyed that he'd come to the door, and said I wasn't allowed to go out the front door where the neighbours could see. I was to go out the back. With it being a terrace house, I had to carry my case from the back of the house to the end of the street, around the corner to the front of the street, then wait until John turned around and saw me waiting.

I was home a week or so when [I learnt] that Dr Amy Robinson was needing a maid for about ten weeks until the 99 year lease on their beautiful big home in about two acres of grounds would be up, and they would be moving out.

'Ingleside' was the sort of home where I would have loved to have worked all my working life. Such homes belonged to the gentry, which they were. There were three floors, about eight bedrooms, dining-room, morning-room (nursery from an earlier day), a butler's pantry, a conservatory full of beautiful scented flowers leading off from the lounge; these were just a few of the parts of the beautiful house. The big beautiful dining-room had a long polished table that would have seated about two dozen people, with lovely silverware and candelabra centrepieces. It was used only once while I was there; they used the morning room for meals most of the time.

They still had two gardeners, a housekeeper-cook and had had two maids; one had left to get married. I was replacing the second, who I think had got another job; I expect they knew they'd all be finished in a few weeks' time. Dr Amy Robinson, who was due to retire, lived there with her crippled brother whose legs had not grown with his body. She was a spinster, and they were both lovely people and very good to work for. They gave me many things near the end …

Cissie married in 1935 and went on to have three children. She died in 2007.

Marian Isobel Taylor

Nursery Maid and General Servant

Born in 1908 near Gateshead in County Durham, Marian Taylor was the daughter of an artist who also worked as a clerk. The family moved to London in 1928 and Marian went into domestic service soon after. She worked first as a nursery maid and later as a general maid. Marian's main employer in the 1930s was Mrs Hill-Smith, who lived at Abbotsbury in Barnet Lane, Elstow, Bedfordshire. There were three other servants in the household.

This extract is taken from an unpublished biography, *The Singing Centenarian*, written by her niece Anne Simmonds and is reproduced with her kind permission.

One evening, us staff were able to foil a gang of burglars when Mr and Mrs Hill-Smith had gone out for dinner. As there was a good fire in the morning-room at the front of the house, May invited the others to go and sit in there. Officially, we were supposed to sit in the servants' hall.

Fairly late in the evening, the front door bell rang. There was stained glass in the windows of the hall so when Winifred went to answer the door, she could see that there were four or five men outside. Before answering, she came and told us. I came into the hall and was 'doing the fire' and May hovered in the doorway of the morning-room.

Winifred opened the door and when the man asked for Mr Hill-Smith, she asked if he had an appointment: "Is Mr Hill-Smith expecting you?"

He began to bluster and said, "Is Mr Hill-Smith at home?"

Winifred asked, "Do you have a card, sir? I will inquire if the master will see you."

He did not have a card and was getting very threatening. Then suddenly both myself and Winifred were startled by a high, rather querulous voice from the morning-room saying, "What is the problem, Winifred? Shall I send for the police?"

Then May appeared and said Mrs 'Hill' was asking what the problem was. At this, the man began to back away and Winifred shut the door and bolted it. We all breathed a sigh of relief. The high querulous voice had been May imitating a previous employer! I ran through to the back and told the cook to bolt the back door as there were suspicious characters around.

A little later, there was a gentle knock at the kitchen door. Ada called, "Who is it?" and got the reply "Arthur". Arthur Smith was the gardener who lived in the lodge by the gate. He was allowed in and he asked if we were all right. His wife had been upstairs drawing the curtains and had seen two cars full of men coming in through the gates without lights on. She had run down and told Arthur and he had gone round by the kitchen garden and garage to get to the house without being seen from the drive. He was glad to find that we had vanquished the burglars. Winifred stayed up until Mr and Mrs Hill-Smith returned and told them the story implying that May was plumping up the cushions in the morning-room and checking the fire, and I had been checking the fire in the hall. Mr Hill-Smith was very grateful to us all.

[*During the 1930s, Marian also filled in for a friend at another house working for the Findsey family.*]

[My friend] Gladys was going home to the north to look after her mother and asked me to keep her job open for her. This was one of the times that I was at home so I jumped at the chance.

[I was working for] a Mr Del Gardo with his married daughter Mrs Findsey and her husband and two sons and also her two unmarried brothers Mr Frank and Mr Alan. It was a tall house with a basement. There was an old cook who had been there for years and had rows of smelly old slippers under the kitchen table. There was no set time for meals for the staff, we just had to find what we could and eat it. I can remember eating cold fried fish for breakfast!

The "useful" maid had been with the family for years and helped make the beds but did very little else. I had to share a very smelly bedroom with her. I thought someone must have upset the "Po" [chamber-pot] and not bothered to wash the mat afterwards! There was also a between maid who waited on the cook but did none of the other work so I was expected to do far more than my fair share of the work.

Mrs Findsey would ring the bell and I would run up the stairs to the first floor sitting room where she would ask me to fetch a clean handkerchief. So I had to run up to the third floor for the hankie but I had to give it to her on a silver salver so I had to go down to the basement to get the salver, and then back up to the first floor to present the handkerchief. When cleaning the bathroom,

I was curious about an old Trilby hat that hung on the back of the door. When I asked about it, I was told that Mr Findsey wore it in the bath to stop his hair curling!

I was often left on my own on a Sunday to heat the soup and serve the midday meal. Each of the five, Mr and Mrs Findsey, Mr Alan, Mr Frank and Mr Del Gardo had to have their own tiny butter dish with a few curls of butter and individual cruets as well as all the usual plates and cutlery. Before serving the sweet I had to clear the table of all these tiny dishes using a long wooden tray. I always had rather short arms and the tray was very long so it used to jab into my neck as I reached for the dishes while balancing the tray on my shoulder.

Once, one of them moved suddenly, I jerked as the tray hit my neck and the butter rolls fell onto Mr. Findsey's greasy curls! I was trying to get them without anyone noticing but Mr Frank saw and burst out laughing saying, "Good old Taylor! I've wanted to put butter on old Findsey's curls for years!" Mrs Findsey was very cross and told her brother, "Frank, be silent!" They were all frightened of Mrs Findsey.

Following her father's death in 1940, Marian and her mother ran a boarding house, mainly for soldiers . After the war, she became a nursery teacher in a private school until she retired at 60. She died in 2008, days after her hundredth birthday.

Dolly Davey

General Servant, Parlourmaid and Lady's Maid

Born in 1913 in Thornaby-on-Tees, Dolly Davey (née Sleeth) had four sisters and two brothers. She was the youngest of the family and always yearned for adventure. In 1930, she took a bus to London to begin a job in domestic service.

This extract is taken from her memoir, *A Sense of Adventure* which was published in 1980 as a result of an oral history project with the SE1 People's History Project. It is reproduced with the kind permission of Jane Mace, the former editor of the project.

It was the futility of it, you know, that made me want to come away. Some of the girls who came out of school went into the factories, or they went to look after babies for the richer people in town. We did have quite a few big houses in the area, and there was quite a bit of domestic work to be had; if it wasn't in the close area, it was in the next town, or the town after that. You could get farm work. But my parents didn't want me to do any of those things …

I was at the impressionable age when other girls had things. I had things I wanted, but I couldn't have real luxuries that I would have liked to have bought myself. I had the necessities of life, but I wanted to buy lisle stockings which were in fashion at the time, and quite expensive at about one and elevenpence a pair. (I was wearing black woollen stockings) … By that time, there wasn't any work for the men in the town – 1929. My father was out of work. I said, "I not only need clothes, I need to have something to make me independent." They couldn't afford to give me a lot of pocket money. They gave me what they could. But I wanted to be independent. My friends had different home lives to me; they were more free than I was. I felt I was being smothered …

I was 17 when I found myself a job through the *Thornaby Gazette*. I wrote off for it, and they sent my fare. I had to accept the job, otherwise send the money back. So I said to my father, "I've got this job, and I'm going." He said, "Not if I know it." So I arranged for an early morning coach to travel from Stockton to

London, and I said to him the night before, "Well, dad, I've arranged to go on the 7 o'clock coach in the morning. I won't be here when you get up."

He was astounded. He was upset. I know he was upset. I went in to see my mother, and she said, "Well, all right, if you intend going, make sure you don't get yourself into trouble." That was her main worry. And my father said, "If you do good for yourself, you'll do good for us." He said, "Just keep in touch with us. Don't get lost. Don't go with strange boys." All the same ritual. Don't do this, don't do that.

I had to do it that way, otherwise I'd never have got away. I'd have ended up an old maid, with no future in front of me. There was nothing else but marriage in those days. It was a way out.

It was really and truly a sense of adventure. I wanted to do something that nobody else in the town had done. I was about the first one to leave and come to London ... I just had my suitcase, and I walked across the bridge into Stockton. It was only a little walk. I got a coach at the corner by the Empire Theatre in Stockton High Street ...

It was quite dark when I got to Victoria. I felt a bit bewildered. I was looking for these people and asking for them. When they came up, they had a car, and they took me to their house in Streatham. The first night, I was allowed to retire early. I didn't start work, because it was pretty late. Of course, I started my full duties the next day – and it was really terrifying! But I wouldn't admit that I was terrified.

The father was a dentist. I had to do the housework, and then take the child to the park. I wasn't sure what was expected, or whether I would come up to standard, not having ever had a house like this to look after. It was big, and it was also in my estimation very richly furnished, and I was a bit afraid of it, because I'd been used to good old furniture.

We'd only ever had the carpet and good furniture in the front room. They had a sweeper. People didn't always have a sweeper; they had to get down and brush and pan.

She didn't stipulate any time to do the work in, but it was certain rooms at certain days. As a general domestic, you had to fit in the washing, cooking and cleaning; [and] also take the child out for walks. So it was a pretty hefty job. By the time the evening came, you didn't feel like doing anything. You just went to bed, and went to sleep, and that was it. I had a room upstairs, next to the child's room. I had it on my own, but it wasn't on my own – because it was open to everyone. I couldn't lock myself in. I had to keep on call to the child, in case she woke up in the night. Very often she did, and she would come in and say she wanted something or she was lonely, or she wanted someone to read to her. Children do, at all different times in the night. I suppose she'd always, since she'd been born, had somebody looking after her. But I wasn't a nanny, and I wasn't used to children. It did appal me sometimes, when she woke in the middle of the night, and I thought something was wrong with her, and it wasn't. It was just that she'd woken up.

Not having the lock on the door, I felt I had no privacy. If the lady of the house had wanted to come into my room, or even the man, I couldn't have stopped them. I had no way to stop it, if it did happen. I often wondered to myself, "Well, what do I do if it does happen?" Especially with the man of the house. It never happened to me, fortunately, but I had that fear at the back of my mind. After being at home like I had.

When I came to London, first of all I felt on the crest of the wave. I thought it was wonderful. I joined the Young Women's Christian Association that used to be in the High Street in Streatham, above a shop, and I used to go there on my days off. They were very, very good. It was a very good idea for girls, who really wanted to keep themselves good, you know? (In those days a lot did come down here, even then, with ideas of just having a good time). They were nearly all domestic servants who used to go there. You'd talk about the people you worked for. You could talk about them to your heart's content, because no-one was there to criticise you. You could tell the truth about them, which really relieved your feelings. One girl I met there, she had a pretty tough job too, in that she was on call day and night with an invalid woman; and she was in a similar position to me – only mine was a child that was always wanting.

It was a very wearing job. I even had the dental surgery to clean, and you know what they're like. You had to be scrupulous. So I decided, or rather they decided for me, when the little girl told them I slapped her. I think it's rather funny now, but at the time I didn't, I thought it was appalling. I took her out one day into the park, and I did get a bit cross with her, but I didn't smack her, and of course the mother naturally believed the child before she believed me. So she gave me a week's notice. I'd been there six months, I should say. You were just the servant: were you to be trusted, or weren't you? I felt that I wasn't trusted. I felt very upset about it.

They waited all day after the child had told them, until I'd served the evening meal, and called me into the sitting room. "Now, we don't allow anyone to slap her." I denied it. But I was only the hired help, wasn't I? and my word wasn't to be believed.

She was that type of person – nasty. I didn't have much respect for her. I had gone there for a job and I had made up my mind that I would do my best for whoever I would work for. I was doing my best: and then to be accused of doing something that I would never dream of doing: I suppose we had learned to accept that they were higher up than we were, in my estimation. See, they were people with money; and you just accepted it, that they just lazed about and did nothing all day.

I went to the Christian Association, and I explained the situation to them, and the lady was kind enough to say, "Well, don't worry about it. We'll find you something by the time you have to leave there." And she did! She had got in touch with some other people on the South side of Streatham Common, and got me this other job.

Well then, each job that I had after than was easier. I always got a reference from each one, except that one. I wasn't in any one too long, because I was only here about four years before I got married. But each job I had, it seemed that something happened that took the people away from me, not me from the people. The second job I had, the people went back to India with relatives. He was an Indian High Court judge; an Englishman, but he worked in the Indian courts. I liked them. They were very nice people. I was a general domestic in that house, too; but I was treated as a friend, not as a domestic. They were very good to me. I didn't wait on them; I just served meals and I didn't have to stand in the dining room.

Next job, you see, they got me because they were leaving. They found me another job, in Forest Hill, in a boarding house. It wasn't as nice as working for the second family. They had no children. It was entirely different. I had all the rooms to do, for the lodgers. (Lodgers, we called them then, not boarders; nothing so posh as boarders, then!) They used to come home for an evening meal, which I had to help prepare. We never got to bed before 11, 12 o'clock at night. I was the only one working there. The landlady was more often out than she was in.

From the boarding house, I went to the judge in Chelsea. That was a really nice family, a really good family. I was a parlour maid. They were badly in need of a parlour maid, and although I hadn't done any work of that type, cook said they would train me. That was the place I liked best. I was parlour maid there, but I also did lady's maid duties – which gave me a good training for the next job I had, where I was entirely a lady's maid. There was a cook, and there were housemaids, and there was the usual muck-in, you know: do this, do that sort of maid – which meant that I only had to be there for meals, and be in the dining room when meals were served, hand dishes round, and stand there and listen and say nothing. Believe me, the things you heard would turn your hair blue, over the dinner table! Especially when they were having dinner parties. It was upper-class gossip.

They had a daughter called Beshe. She was very fussy; she bathed, oh, perhaps five, six times a day, and I always had to have her bath running. In fact, it was never empty, I don't think … I'd have to wait there for her coming out, and see that her clothes were done, ready for putting on. I used to do her personal washing. Every five minutes she was changing her clothes and bathing. She would have been about my own age, about 18. They were the type that would have coming-out parties.

They had books in the house, but we weren't allowed in the library. A lot of people didn't think that you should be educated, if you were a servant. I already had an education before I came to London, so it didn't worry me. I brought my own books, so I kept them in my room. One thing about it, being a parlour maid, I did have a room on my own. Whereas lower servants had to share a room.

I got on very well there. Then, they decided they were leaving; so I got my own job, the next one. I saw it advertised. The cook said they would give me a reference, if I needed one (because it was all left down to the cook and housekeeper there).

I graduated from parlour maid to lady's maid, in Belgravia … I worked for Lady Beauchamp, whose house was in Beauchamp Place. She was a lovely person … When I went after this job, I explained that I had done a little work as a lady's maid, but I wasn't trained. So the lady said, "Well, we'll see what you can do. We'll give you a trial." And then she gave me a trial – and she was pleased with me.

We all got different levels of wages – but we never knew what we each got. We never brought up about it, strangely enough. They were called into the master's room when I worked over at Chelsea, for the judge. When I worked for Lady Beauchamp, it [the pay] was sent to us with the butler. He used to bring it on a tray.

We did wear uniform. In one place I think we did get a new uniform at Christmas – because of the change from black and white to brown and coffee colour. That was our present one year in one house. I had the feeling that they didn't think maids should have Christmas presents. I can't remember having anything different to that one time.

The under-maids – the kitchen maids and that – used to come and go like anybody's business. They were there one week and then the next week they wouldn't be there. You never knew they were leaving. You didn't have the companionship with the other maids that you should have had, that you would have today. They didn't mix. When I was finished in the dining room I'd go down to cook and say, "They've said they didn't want me any more tonight." She'd say, "Well, alright, you can go to bed," and I would disappear. So I never met any of the others.

When I left home, when I finally made up my mind and I had convinced my parents that I was leaving, the first thing my mother made me do was make sanitary pads, out of terry towelling. I had to stitch them all myself. You folded them cornerways and then you pinned them on to a belt or tape with safety pins. They rubbed: and if you couldn't change often enough, if you were kept in the dining room and you felt, "Oh goodness me, if I could only get out and get changed." You had to suffer agonies through this chafing. It was very uncomfortable.

I wasn't allowed to hang my washing out in the garden. That was forbidden. But the family's things, they could go out. They used to have the woman come in to do their washing, and I was to do the fine things of Lady Beauchamp's. That was one thing she was very, very particular about, ironing. She used to wear these cotton interlock vests, and if you had a crease in them you had to iron and iron it until it came out. She would show me continuously how to iron these things, but I could never iron them without creasing them …

You had the old flat iron. What we used to do was have a piece of brown paper and we used to rub it all over with salt, and put some bathbrick over the top of that; (like a powdered brick, that we used to clean the baths with). It didn't have any smell at all. It was just like a powder. And you'd sprinkle that over the top of the salt, and as you took the iron off the gas you'd rub it over this paper. It used to be like silver at the bottom, it came out so clean.

I once scorched a very, very lovely pair of crepe de chine French knickers belonging to her. I was ironing them, and instead of trying the iron out on something else first, which I usually did, I grabbed at these pants, put them on the table (we didn't have an ironing board) and whizz! right through! Oh, I really didn't know how to go and tell her. I felt sure she'd sack me on the spot.

When I finally did pluck up courage and say to her, "My Lady, I've done something terrible," she said, "What have you done, Dorothy?" I said, "I have burnt your French knickers." So she said, "Which ones?" When I showed her these cream ones with coffee-coloured lace, "Oh, it's alright," she said. "It was an old pair anyway."

I really felt relieved: because I was sure she was going to sack me – or I'd have to pay for them. They cost more than the week's wages I got. I got eleven shillings a week, and you couldn't possibly pay for things like that. That's why you had to be so careful. If they had said to you, "You'll have to pay for this," we'd have had no wages for months ...

In her own way, she used to really adore me, because I could do everything for her. I could dress her hair, and I could do her clothes. I don't know whether I'm singing my own praises or not – but I knew how to look after her. It was not the nouveau riche, like my first job; it was the aristocracy, the rich rich. There's such a difference between them. If you've mixed with them, you see the difference from people who've become rich, and want to lord it over everybody. People who are born rich, they accept you.

I enjoyed it. It was different. I wasn't serving my mother and father. I wasn't being victimised, let's say – which I thought at the time: "My mother is an invalid, my father will be an invalid eventually. Am I going to stay there for ever, and become an old maid?" Lying in bed, I used to think about it, and I'd think, "No, never. That isn't for me – looking after elderly parents, and not ever seeing anything of life." It wasn't for me; and I'd made up my mind to it. Maybe I was hard, I don't know. I didn't feel hard. They had my sisters living in the next town.

When I first came down, I was being paid two and sixpence a week, all found. I never could send anything back home; even in my last job (which was a classy job) I only got eleven shillings a week. That was supposed to be a good wage. My mother always said, though, and my father, "As long as you're alright, you don't have to send anything home," because they didn't need it. You see, they were getting old. They were eighty, and they had enough for their needs. They didn't need anything out of my pittance.

When I first came to London, it wasn't my intention to stay. It was a stepping stone to further adventure. When I came, I thought, "Good. Now I'm on my way. The first stepping stone is London. I'll work. I'll earn some money, I'll go to the shipping office. I'll see if I can't be a stewardess on board ship." Not any old ship, I didn't intend. It had to be a good ship, where I could meet good people. I suppose I wanted to better myself.

I think what sparked it off was my father telling me about his brothers and sisters who had gone abroad. He had sisters in New Zealand. He had brothers and sisters in Canada. They came to visit occasionally when we were children, and I think it fascinated me. It really got at me. It seemed so far away.

When the 1926 strike came, people were emigrating, and I said to my father, "Why don't we?" He said they were too old. I said, "Well, I'm not. Could I go?" He said, "Oh, no." He wouldn't even let me emigrate to my uncle in Canada, his own family. So of course, that was in my mind, and when I came here, I fully intended being on the high seas. I put my name down on the shipping line; but of course nothing ever came of it.

When I was working in this Beauchamp Place, Frederick came along. He was working for a delivery firm; a small continental firm in Wardour Street. He used to deliver caviar and all lovely exotic foods – none of which I ever ate, or got a chance to, actually. We got friendly, and on my days out we would make a date where to meet.

I often think to myself, "What did he see in me?" I was only a domestic servant. He was out in the limelight, sort of thing, out in the world. He was free to do what he wanted. What did he see in me? He's often said to me, he thought I was untouchable, something out of this world; and yet I thought *he* was out of this world, because he had this freedom. He lived at home with his parents, and I was like a bird in a cage, when I wanted to be out. You haven't got your freedom. You do have everything – if you get the right kind of job, like the last one I had. You were considered, you were thought about, you weren't just plummeted into the cellar from somewhere; but you weren't free.

She didn't want me to leave. She said I could still carry on working. She said I had served her very well, and if I ever did want to work again, she would give me a reference. I felt quite proud. Of course, when I suggested going daily, when I married Fred, he said no, he didn't want his wife to work. And that, believe it or not, went on for years and years. He'd never let me work. I stayed at home, and I had the children. When the war years came, I did work. From then on, he's never said no. The first work I ever did was in the NAAFI in Kennington Road. I only had two children then, and they were at school.

Elsie

Housemaid

Elsie was born in Lincolnshire in 1920. She worked as a housemaid for four years at Holbeck Manor, before being called up into the WAAF for war service. This extract is taken from her memories of her time in domestic service, as told to her granddaughter.

I left school the day I turned 14 (in 1934) to look after my younger brother who was very ill. George could not be left alone and both Mum and Dad worked on their farm so could not care for him. As George got better, I helped my father on the farm but by the time I was 16, my parents could not afford to keep me. So I had to look for a job and I was due to start work as a nanny at the home of a policeman but my mother felt that I was too young to care for a child and would not let me go. A family friend who worked at Holbeck Manor visited and told me that a housemaid's position was available there. I was interviewed by Miss Neal-Green [the employer's daughter] and was accepted onto the staff.

The working day as a housemaid was from 6.45am–7pm and I received wages of 28 shillings per calendar month. This was a generous wage as I boarded at the manor and all my meals and a uniform were provided for me. All the staff were fed well and we ate the same food as our employers. My uniform as a housemaid was a black dress, which I had to wear with a white mob cap and black stockings in the morning. In the afternoon, I had to change to tan stockings with a band worn around my head. I also had to have different pairs of shoes for morning and afternoon.

As a junior housemaid, my duties were mainly related to cleaning the bedrooms of the house but I also waited at the table for meals. If I was not required, I was allowed to remain in my room. One morning task was to clean the bedroom fire grates, a job at which I became very proficient and also very quiet. I was able to clean the grate, refill a coal bucket and relight the fire in the bedroom of Mrs Neal-Green, all without waking her. My ability to do this was valued so much that when I was promoted to head housemaid, I was still required to clean the grate in her room. My employer always treated me very well, describing me as 'a good and faithful child' and when I was suffering badly from hayfever, she even asked her own doctor to travel up from Harley Street to see if anything could be done to alleviate my symptoms.

Housemaid duties also included assisting with service at mealtimes and during a party one evening, I had been helping to clear the table. The guests had opened several bottles of wine and these were cleared with each course but the domestic staff had been consuming the alcohol left in the bottles. I was sent to clear the table but had to return to the kitchen to ask another person to help as I was seeing double and could not pick up the plates.

A girl called Nellie, who was the same age as me, was doing the washing up and was given a glass which contained all the dregs from the leftover bottles. She became so inebriated that she began re-washing the pots she had already washed. Nellie shouted, "I love washing up!" and started singing so loudly, we had to hurry her to bed so that the employers did not hear her. In the morning, she had a headache and told the others, including me, that we were 'buggers' for giving her the drink.

I was very happy in domestic service and were it not for the Second World War, I would not have left. I worked at Holbeck Manor for four years in total until I was called up for the WAAF.

Lily Kerry

Housemaid

Lily Kerry (née Bird) was born in 1923 in Bury St Edmunds, the eldest of two children. Her father worked for the council, laying pavements, while her mother had been a maid in a sanatorium before her marriage. When Lily went into service, her second employers were the Misses Boby, who in their youth had been used to having servants do everything for them. By 1937, they were still living in their large Victorian house but by now they had to do the cooking and some of the cleaning themselves, possibly because of deteriorating financial circumstances.

This extract is taken from an interview given to the author by Lily Kerry.

In 1937, I turned 14 and left school. I was still just a child and I didn't know what job I wanted to do. In Bury St Edmunds where I was born and raised, there was a clothing factory and a few hand laundries where you could get work. But I knew I didn't want to go in a factory. Some of my friends did that but I couldn't imagine sitting at a sewing machine all day or ironing in a laundry! So it was just expected that I would go into service.

At 14, you didn't usually go to a place and live in. My Mum's neighbour's daughter had to though; she went into service when she was 14, right away to sleep in, but she was working in a great big house in the country which was different really. I was glad I didn't have to do that.

My first job in service was for Mrs Culley who lived in a detached house in Bury St Edmunds. Mrs Culley's daughter was my teacher at school and my Mum got me the job. I didn't have an interview or anything because Miss Culley knew me from school. As far as I can remember, my Mum said I had a job with Mrs Culley and that was that. I just did as I was told!

The house had four bedrooms, a dining-room, a sitting-room and a kitchen. The work wasn't hard, it was quite easy really. I just did all sorts of little jobs in the house. There was an enormous garden so a lot of the time in the better weather, I used to go with Mrs Culley and do jobs in the garden. To me, that wasn't work at all. It was enjoyment because I liked gardening so much.

I'd get there about half past eight in the morning. They'd just had their breakfast so I automatically went in and washed up the breakfast things. There was linoleum on the bedroom floors and rugs, and a carpet in the drawing-room. If I was cleaning a particular room, I had to take the rugs outside and give them a good shake, and bang on them with a stick sometimes. Then I had lunch with them and I ate exactly the same food. Later on, I always had a cup of tea with them before I went home about mid-afternoon.

You didn't work long hours for that type of job. The Culleys were nice people and they treated me like one of them, not like a servant. I stayed in touch with Mrs Culley's granddaughter for years and years, even after she moved to America. She was a lifelong friend.

When I turned 16, I was expected to go and live in as a servant. That was because my Mum had done that when she was a young woman. We were living in a two bedroom house and my Mum wanted my room for my brother who was two years younger than me. As I was the eldest, I had to leave. That was the way of it. It was fair enough but I knew of girls who went to the factories or the laundries with three or four siblings at home, still living in just a two bedroom house. That would have been very overcrowded. Before I left, my brother slept in a bed in my parents' bedroom. My future husband's eldest sisters Phyllis and Hilda had to do the same thing because he was one of six. But they had to go and live in at 14.

I didn't really mind leaving Mrs Culley's. I don't think she would have wanted me to stop longer because they were used to having somebody straight from school for a couple of years, then probably she had somebody younger again. They didn't have to pay so much for a girl who'd just left school.

I went to work for the Misses Boby [*pronounced Bo-bee*], still in Bury St Edmunds, but living in. Again, my Mum must have found out about the job. I remember an old lady coming to our house and she interviewed me, I suppose. She was one of the Misses Boby and she talked to me for a bit, then told me I'd got the job.

The Bobys had been business people and I suppose at one time they had been a wealthy family. But that was long before I was there because I worked for two elderly sisters – Miss Ethel and Miss Daisy. They had a married sister who lived in London but I don't remember any men about the place. Joan, my future husband's sister, was already in service there so I wasn't on my own. There was also a young fellow who came once a week to clean their boots and shoes, and the knives, plus a gardener who came once a week. Mr Rose, his name was. They had a lovely walled garden with a lawn and flowers all around it.

The Boby family had obviously been used to having servants all their lives. Miss Daisy and Miss Ethel had never done any work to our knowledge but they never talked about their lives when they were young. Now they were having to do bits of housework for themselves. Miss Daisy did the cooking, which sounds strange but she did, and Joan helped her. Miss Ethel was the one who did the shopping and she helped me make the beds.

I don't know how old they were but to us, they were very old-fashioned. I don't suppose for a minute they were older than their sixties even. They never ever wore anything but long, tweedish skirts, high blouses with a brooch and three-quarter length jackets. Never ever wore anything else, Sundays, weekdays or anything. They always looked as though they were pulled in tight.

They lived in a lovely, big three storey house. Long before we worked there, things must have been very different because they had a drawing-room, a dining-room, and a sort of sitting-room. Twenty years before, the drawing-room and dining-room were probably used when their parents were alive, but never in all the time we were there. They just looked like something out of a museum.

There were a lot of rooms, there was a big kitchen with an enormous room in the middle which wasn't used for anything. In this middle room, there was a huge fireplace and a thing called a spit on the top. Years ago, they used to cook a great big piece of joint or an animal on it. I can't imagine it ever being used but it must have been fifty or a hundred years before that. We had to go down the hall through this room into the kitchen, then there was another side room which they called the office, I think. But it wasn't used for anything; it just had furniture in.

Upstairs, there were six bedrooms plus a little sewing room on the top floor and a nice, big room for Joan and I. That was comfortable with two beds, one up one end of the room, and one the other. There was a chest of drawers and a washstand, just basic things. In those days, you didn't have many personal things of your own and you hadn't got many clothes, that's for sure.

When you went in to the house, there was the front hall with these really nice stairs going up. Joan and I never used the front stairs, we went up and down the back stairs to our bedrooms. There was a side door which led to the little office place, and then the back stairs.

There was a bathroom but they didn't have a bath every day like people do today. Everyone had a washstand and basin in their bedroom. Joan and I were allowed to have a bath in there on a Saturday. I think the water was heated with a sort of geyser. We had to take hot water up to our bedroom and in to Miss Daisy's and Miss Ethel's rooms. They sent their clothes to the laundry to be washed so we didn't see a sign of that. I took my washing home but you didn't have the amount of things that they have today.

They'd got a lavatory indoors but I don't think that was in the bathroom. They'd got one just outside as well. I think they were still using chamber pots in their rooms. There must have been another lavatory that Joan and I used because we didn't use the same one as the Misses Boby.

We had to provide our own uniform which was a white overall and a sort of white cap on our heads. In the afternoon, because I was similar to a housemaid, I wore a navy frock and a little frilly white apron. If people like the doctor came to visit, which was few and far between, I opened the door to them.

We started work at about seven o'clock in the morning and took Miss Daisy and Miss Ethel a cup of tea. I laid the fire in their sitting-room and Joan would do the fire in the kitchen. Although they had electric lights in the house, they still cooked on an old-fashioned range with a coal fire. We had to bring up the coal from the cellar for the coal scuttles by the fireplaces and the range. It was quite heavy work. When we were laying the fires, we had an apron to put on top of the overalls or they wouldn't have stayed white for long.

Before breakfast, Joan and I had to go into prayers. We had to kneel down in front of two dining-room chairs and Miss Ethel read the prayers every morning. You can't imagine it today but they were two real Christian ladies.

I suppose they came down to breakfast at about half past eight. We served it in what I called their sitting-room, where they ate all their meals. The room had great big windows on to the garden and so did their drawing-room. I can't remember such a thing as cereal, but they used to have eggs and toast, and possibly kippers sometimes.

After breakfast, I used to go up and help Miss Ethel make the beds, just their two beds. She'd be one side and I'd be on the other. Joan was always downstairs with Miss Daisy, she used to do the washing up and things like that. Afterwards, I tidied the bedrooms and dusted downstairs. They had a carpet in the drawing-room and also a big glass fish tank, which they called the coral. It was just like a model of a coral beach, but with real coral. I can't remember seeing fish in it but it was one of the things in their drawing-room which was a big attraction in those days.

Although it was a big house, there was just a fire in their sitting-room and another in the kitchen – there were no fires anywhere else. Everywhere was cold in those days, because there was no central heating. We weren't allowed a fire in our room, and we took hot water bottles to bed to keep warm.

We had a break mid-morning when we made ourselves a cup of cocoa or coffee. Then they had lunch pretty well about one o'clock. They were regimented with their times so the place ran like clockwork. They had dinner at lunchtime, a proper cooked meal. I can't remember a meal in the evening, if they had one. I know they had afternoon tea about four o'clock. This was just sandwiches and some cake, and we had it at the same time. We had the same food as them, but during the war, that was all rationed so you didn't have much choice. Although there were lots of bells all in a line in the kitchen from years ago, we never really used them. They just had meals at a certain time and that was it.

I had to take the dinner in for them and I can't remember if I put it on the sideboard or on the table for them but I know whatever they had, we had as well. For dinner, they had the same as three parts of the world had in those days. You had a joint on Sunday, you had it cold on Monday and you had shepherd's pie on Tuesday. On Saturdays, they used to leave Joan and I some apples or other fruit as a bit of a treat. There were no oranges and bananas in the shops then.

We nearly lived on brawn in the war, it was made from pigs' heads and things in a basin and turned out like a little jelly. The brawn was really nice and we ate it cold, in slices. When you think what we lived on then, we were a jolly sight healthier than we are now.

Joan and I ate in the kitchen, separate from Miss Daisy and Miss Ethel. They were different people to Mrs Culley; these two were what I call ladies. But they were good people. Before I went there, before rationing, I remember being told that they used to cook a joint of beef on Boxing Day and take it to the poor people in Eastgate Street not far away.

We were just ordinary common or garden, but they were different. When I look back, we never thought of them being wealthy which they must have been, but it never entered our heads. They lived very plainly and even if there hadn't been rationing, I think they would still have lived very ordinary.

In the afternoons, there wasn't a lot to do so Joan and I used to just sit there by the fire in the kitchen, reading a book or knitting. I used to clean the brasses and all the silver, which took some time. This was just the silver they used every day. I can remember Miss Daisy coming through and seeing me sitting there cleaning it all. And she said, "I can see you're used to work, you're doing that well."

They did all the shopping, we didn't have to help with that. We always had a baker come with the bread, and the milkman with the milk, but nothing else was delivered. The shops in town were in walking distance so Miss Daisy and Miss Ethel didn't have to go far. Their church was only five minutes down the road.

In the evenings, Miss Daisy and Miss Ethel would be in their sitting-room and we'd be in the kitchen. It really was a very quiet house. We'd never be late to bed and they always went to bed in good time. They had hot water bottles put in the bed and in the morning when they got up, they sometimes used that hot water bottle water just to wash with.

Even though they weren't using lots of the rooms, they still had to be dusted. Once a year, they always had spring cleaning; Joan's sister worked there before us, and she used to come to help out. Well, we would start at the top with all those bedrooms. They were never used but they had to be washed and cleaned, the paint was washed and the floors were done.

Miss Daisy had two cats and they went in their sitting-room with them. She used to go to the fish shop and buy the fishes' heads, which you wouldn't dream of buying today because everything's thrown away. She'd come home and cook them for the cats – they were really spoiled!

Looking back, it wasn't a hard job at all. We didn't have to work hard and we were treated very well by the ladies. They went to church every Sunday and on Good Friday. Joan and I went to a different church but we had to go every week. The Misses Boby never ever went away. They lived a very quiet life and never did any entertaining – that's probably why the job seemed so easy!

I was paid about a pound a week, with all my food and board included. The money I earned was mine to keep and I always tried to save a little, even if that was just shillings. In those days, wherever you were, you tried to save for your old age. Once a week, I had Friday afternoon and evening off, and Joan had Saturday afternoon and evening; we just had a week's holiday once a year. On my days off, I always went home to see my Mum and took my washing! I brought it back the next week.

During the war, people were only allowed to keep one servant. When I turned 18 and I signed all the papers like you had to do, Miss Ethel told me that she'd got me deferred from war work and I just didn't think any more about it. Joan was called up and she had to go into the Land Army.

Even after she left, it wasn't hard work as such because they didn't do any entertaining or anything. There was just the two ladies and because of the rationing, you could only do so much. But they wouldn't have managed on their own, not in that big house.

I met Bob, my future husband, through Joan; he was her brother. I only got to see him at weekends or when it was my day off. He would call in to see us sometimes, and then I worked it so I had a week's holiday when he came. But we didn't see a lot of each other because you couldn't have every evening off. Then Bob was called up in 1940 and he was away until 1946; I wrote to him every single afternoon and I used to walk every day to the post office to post my letter.

During the war, Miss Ethel and Miss Daisy's married sister and her family used to come to stay to get away from the bombing for a week or a fortnight at a time. It didn't make much difference to the workload and there was plenty of room for them. Their nephew Raymond came to see his aunts regularly when he was doing some war work locally looking after Italian prisoners. He must have been in his thirties. Master Raymond, we called him. Some of the neighbours used to come down into the cellar with us when the air raid siren went off in the middle of the night and we were all down there together.

Looking back, I might have been a bit lonely when Joan went off to the Land Army but I never thought of it like that, it was just what you did. After she left, somebody else did come to help me but she didn't stop long. She was probably called up as well.

I would have liked to have had time to myself in the evenings but you just accepted that that was how it was. We had to be there in case Miss Daisy or Miss Ethel needed us. If they wanted a drink, we got it for them. In the seven years I worked there, there were never any real problems between me and the Misses Boby. But then I wouldn't have dared to disagree with them or answer them back. They were just very gentle ladies.

Being in domestic service gave me a good idea of what it would be like to run my own house. Bob came home in 1946 and we got married that year; I had been able to build up some savings from my wages. When I got married, Miss Ethel and Miss Daisy gave me one of their antique chests of drawers. It was a good one and I sold it some years later for £20. My daughter told me off and said I shouldn't have parted with it!

When I left, the Misses Boby had a foreign couple go and live there but they didn't last long. Joan went back to work for them when she got married because you couldn't get anywhere to live in those days. She had her first baby there too. They knew her well and they just wanted someone who was reliable.

After I married, I didn't really keep in touch with Miss Daisy and Miss Ethel afterwards but when they died, they left Joan and me £50 each which was a lot of money in those days so they must have thought highly of us.

Lily left domestic service in 1946 when she got married and later had two children. She worked for some time as a home help, but never returned to domestic service.

David Dixon

Houseboy and Cook

Born in Enfield in 1919, David Dixon worked in domestic service in London between December 1936 and February 1940, when he was called up to join the RAF. He started off as a houseboy and, unusually, ended up as a cook.

This extract is taken from correspondence between David Dixon and the author.

I was the eldest of six boys and we lived in a hamlet near Millom in Cumbria, having moved there in 1931. Our mother had lived in Enfield all her life but never returned, and never wanted to. Our father had been wounded in World War One and was not able to work. His only income was a small war pension and any odd jobs he could do. The 1930s was a difficult time to be looking for work and the only jobs available in Millom were at the ironworks or down the iron ore mine, neither of which I wanted to do. Each of us boys needed to move away from the area for better prospects and we were encouraged to look for jobs in the south.

In 1935 at the age of 16, I went to London on a YMCA scheme and was based in the East End. I was keen to get into a job and was sent to a house in Birchington-upon-Sea where I was to be the houseboy. I had no idea what domestic service would be like but that didn't bother me. The lady I was working for had a lot of bridge parties and I did jobs around the house and a bit of cooking, which I liked doing. I'd been taught how to cook when I was in the Scouts. I remember I knew how to cook chips and I fried onions in deep fat but it landed all over the floor!

I wasn't in this first job for very long, only about six weeks. I said I wanted to leave and eventually she decided to sack me. I wasn't happy there because I wasn't treated in the way I'd been used to at home. They didn't treat me badly, they just weren't very kind or considerate, apart from at Christmas. I waited on the family and afterwards we had our own Christmas dinner in the dining room after they'd finished, which had been cooked by some ladies who'd come in especially. I was also very lonely as I was the only servant.

When I left, I went back to the YMCA and they gave me a job in a hostel in Kensington Gardens Square. I worked in the kitchen from January 1936 until November that year. I remember being there when King George V died in January because I went to the lying in state in Westminster Hall and all the shops were decorated in black. Towards the end of 1936, my grandparents were on a visit to London and they came to see me in the hostel. They weren't very happy about me working there because they thought I should be doing something better.

They contacted a cousin of my mother's who knew a man called William Stone. He was a butler for the Sandberg family and he happened to be looking for a houseboy. Mr Stone recommended me for the position so I had an interview with Mr Sandberg who had an office just outside Victoria. I got the job and left the hostel around the same time as King Edward VIII abdicated, moving to the Sandbergs' house on 6 December 1936.

My new employer was a Swedish consulting engineer who had recently made a lot of money by resurrecting a sunken ship called the *Egypt* which was full of gold. He had a wife, three sons and four daughters. The eldest son and daughter were both married and living in their own homes. The second son, Mr Bill, was away from home and the third son, Mr John, was at boarding school. The second and third daughters, Miss Christina and Miss Rosina, lived at home while the youngest, Miss Penelope, was away at school. Mr Sandberg travelled to his office in London daily.

They lived in a newly built property near Edenbridge, Kent called West House. It had a drawing-room, a lounge-hall (which was the most used room), a dining-room, kitchen, scullery, butler's pantry, boot room, ten bedrooms and four bathrooms. During my time there, an extra drawing-room and a servants' annexe were added.

There was a butler (Mr Stone), a cook and a housemaid who lived in, plus several others who came from the village and lived out. We all got on well together and it was much better than being on my own. In fact, the day that I moved in was the same day of the house-warming party so I had to get stuck in straight away. It was quite a good party!

As the houseboy, I was to assist the butler, helping to serve meals, washing up, cleaning shoes, filling coal scuttles, cleaning brasses and any other jobs which came up. My working hours were from 6.30am to 2pm and 4.30pm to 8.30pm. They were long days in service and for this, I was paid 10 shillings per week.

To begin with, I slept in an outside room, next to the garage, but later moved into the servants' annexe. This was made up of three bedrooms, a bathroom and a sort of kitchen-cum-living room. We all lived in that room and ate in there too; we never ate in the kitchen. It had a kitchen fireplace in it too in case the Aga went wrong. They were quite nice rooms, and I had a fireplace in mine so I used to light a fire there. I don't think the Sandbergs ever knew!

Every February, the family went on holiday to the South of France for a month. In my first year of service, Mrs Sandberg arranged for me to go and work as a general servant for her sister who lived a few miles away; the money was better in my pocket than in someone else's. This was a much smaller place than the Sandbergs' house and I learned quite a lot, such as how to fire the Aga properly! There was a sort of footman there but he left when I was there and I ended up doing all sorts of jobs, including a bit of plain cooking. In subsequent years, I was given two weeks' holiday and was able to go home to Millom while the family was away.

I also had Sunday evenings off and a half day on Thursdays. In the afternoons, I regularly walked the Sandbergs' dogs and enjoyed exploring the countryside. On my half day off, I used to go into Edenbridge to the pictures. Eventually, I bought a bicycle on the never-never so I could get out and about more easily. None of my relatives lived round there but one of the maids lived in the village and I became quite friendly with her and her family.

As it turned out, Mr Stone didn't stay long after I started working for the Sandbergs. It was the gardener's job to look after the boiler for the hot water, and when he finished work at four or five o'clock, he always shut it down. A few months after I arrived, in February 1937, the family were out to dinner one evening and arrived back very late. I was already in bed but the girls all decided they wanted baths. Eventually, there was no hot water for Mr Sandberg. This was at one o'clock in the morning and Mr Stone roused me to go and see Mr Sandberg. He was in a furious rage and had quite an altercation with Mr Stone, blaming me for the loss of the hot water. I can remember his words: "When I want hot water, I want hot water!" That was the only time that I saw him lose his temper. He and Mr Stone almost had a fight and I think that's why Mr Stone left.

A few weeks afterwards, Mr Stone wrote and offered me a job as a footman where he was working. I'm not sure why but I showed the letter to Mrs Sandberg. She persuaded me to stay and said they would deal with Mr Stone. They ended up sending him a solicitor's letter and that was the last I heard of him. I wasn't really tempted to go because I preferred working at the Sandbergs' house to anywhere else.

Mr Stone was replaced by Harold Foster, who was quite good in his job as butler. He had a wife, Kath, and they lived in a cottage in the village. She did some of the cooking and when I went into the RAF, she took over as cook.

The Sandbergs also owned a cottage at Grasmere in the Lake District and in May 1937, I was driven up by the chauffeur and accommodated in a lodging house nearby. We were there for about a month, during which time I was the general dogsbody in the cottage and even did some cooking for them. I think it was then they realised I was able to cook. I learned this skill when I was in the Scouts and I had been able to practise further in the YMCA kitchens. This was my first visit to the central Lake District and I loved it. Unfortunately, I was not near enough to come home for a visit.

On a later trip to Grasmere, the eldest daughter Evalina visited and while she was there, she bought a pet lamb from a local farmer. I was given the job of taking the lamb in a cage on the train to London. The cage was placed in the guard's van and I had to visit it throughout the journey to look after the lamb. On arrival at Euston, I took a taxi to Victoria and then on the train to Oxted – still with the lamb in the cage. That was a different experience altogether!

We used to go up once or twice each year to Grasmere and it was during one such visit in 1938, I was offered the job of cook at £1 per week. I don't know why the previous cook left but I wanted to get on. It was quite unusual to go from being a houseboy to a cook but it was a good step up in wages; I only got 10 bob as a houseboy.

As the cook, I didn't have any other help in the kitchen. It was a nice kitchen, quite modern, with an Aga and sinks for washing up. The butler's pantry was next door. To make sure I got up in time, Mrs Sandberg told me that she wanted a pot of tea at half past six in the morning. So I had to take it up to her bedroom and really that was to make certain I was up! That was alright, I then had to service the Aga and scrub the kitchen floor, putting newspapers down as it dried. The next job was preparing breakfast for the family and the servants. Mrs Sandberg usually came down to the kitchen at about half past nine or ten o'clock and we discussed the day's menu and any other matters.

I made breakfast and lunch for them at home. Breakfast was usually boiled eggs, Mr Sandberg always had them lightly boiled. That was the main thing they had, they didn't have bacon and eggs, or porridge or anything like that. I recall some kedgeree on one occasion. I also used to bake the cakes for tea – I don't remember the Sandbergs ever having dinner parties but they often invited people to tea. I was very proud to have baked the cakes for Mrs Churchill when she came to tea one day.

When I turned 20 in 1939, like all 20 year olds, I had to register for military service. I was with the family for more than three years before I was called up on 7 February 1940 and had to leave straight away. Working in domestic service was an interesting experience but even if there hadn't been a war, I don't think I would have stayed. I had other ambitions, I still had ideas about joining the church but at that time, I hadn't got the education I needed. Mrs Sandberg encouraged me to go to the eight o'clock service at church every Sunday morning and she helped me to foster my vocation. I kept in touch with the Sandbergs for a long time afterwards as they were such a lovely family.

My last visit to West House was in 1967 during my time as the vicar of a parish near Workington. Mrs Sandberg was then of a great age and being cared for. Her first words to me were, "I don't believe it, I don't believe it!"

After the war, David returned to Cumbria and worked in a tannery, then in a factory doing screen printing, before moving to Sellafield. He later married and was ordained as a vicar in 1958.

Daphne Jones

Maidservant

Daphne Jones was born in 1926 in Woolwich, south-east London. In June 1940, shortly after the disaster of Dunkirk, she was evacuated with her brother Colin to a small village near Plymouth. Daphne was 14 and Colin was almost nine. They hoped to be placed in a home together but instead were both billeted in very unsatisfactory homes. After a few weeks, Daphne was moved to a better one, but very soon, as she was by now the oldest in her class, she wanted to get a job.

Her new foster mother managed to get her a job in the small town of Ivybridge five miles away, as a live-in maid servant in a private house at 10 shillings a week. Daphne's brother Colin visited her by bus a few times and she managed to see him once a week for a while. She was dreadfully unhappy and left after five months, returning to London and to the bombing which she found more congenial.

Daphne recalled her experiences in an interview with Colin, from which this extract is taken.

The work was hard and the hours long, but by far the worst part of it was the loneliness and homesickness. The couple in the house were Mr and Mrs Brendon. Although he was barely middle-aged, the man of the house was not involved in any work of any sort and seemed a bag of nerves. Whether this was caused by his experience in the First World War, I don't know. It was she who was in charge.

My wages were ten shillings a week and I had Wednesday afternoon off and most of Sunday when I went to church like everybody else in those days. They gave me a tiny bedroom right at the top of the house and I was hardly ever off duty. Sometimes well after 10 o'clock, she would say to me, "You can go to bed now, Daphne."

Each morning I got up at 6.30am and began the day by clearing out the ashes and making up the fires in all the rooms. I did not do the cooking but had to help in the kitchen. My younger brother remembers that I had linen bags of homemade cheese hanging up over the sink.

Because of the intense loneliness, I was so thankful that at church I met up with a girl of my age, Olive and we became friends. I relied upon her for advice. One day, Mrs Brendon told me that they were going to Scotland for a week and that I was to sleep in the house of the gardener and his wife. However, she said, "You must come to this house each day and do your work!"

Being so young, green and obedient, I did just that. Every day I went to the house and did all the cleaning conscientiously. They arrived back on the Sunday and on the Wednesday morning while I was working with her, I asked her if she wanted some jobs done that day and she said, "Oh, I don't know, I'll let you know this afternoon!"

Plucking up courage that I did not know I had, I said, "Perhaps you have forgotten that Wednesday is my afternoon off?"

She was astonished! "What! You have just had a week's holiday and you expect to have the afternoon off!"

The disappointment ran through my body as a physical pain – I remember it going right down to my fingertips! I went back to my room and sobbed, then I wrote a letter to my mother pouring out all my feelings. By return of post, I received a letter from Mum saying, "Give in your notice and you must come back to London and risk the bombs."

What a relief! But then I realised that I had no idea how people gave in their notice! My friend Olive came to the rescue. She had seen an American film so she told me what to do.

"You have to say 'Take a week's notice' and then you have to break all the china in the kitchen," she said.

I protested that I could not possibly do that.

"Yes, you can, and you must break all that china."

I went back to my room and I tried rehearsing, but whatever way I said it, it sounded very rude so I toned it down a bit. Then the next morning when I was alone with the master, I said, "Would you please take a week's notice."

He was hard of hearing so I had to say it louder. This time it came out, before I could stop it, as "Take a week's notice."

The master was mortified and began to shake. He called up the stairs to his wife to come down at once. Then I had to say it again, "Take a week's notice."

She was aghast, "Well, there are ways and ways of saying things and that is not at all a nice way!"

Needless to say, I did not dare to break anything! So quite soon, I was on the way to London but feeling dreadful having left my smaller brother behind in a home where he was so unhappy.

Back home in Eltham, I was able to get a few jobs in shops and offices, but most nights I was off in the black-out and raids to night-school where I learned shorthand and typing which gave me a proper career as a secretary.

Amy Jones

Nursemaid and General Servant

Born in 1930 in Ton-y-refail, Mid Glamorgan, South Wales, Amy Jones was sent into service at the age of 13 and 11 months, ostensibly to work as a nursemaid. Instead, all her duties revolved around cooking and cleaning, and the experience marked an extremely unhappy time in her life.

This extract is taken from correspondence between Amy Jones and the author.

When I was about 12 or 13 years old, our teacher asked us what we wanted to do on leaving school. At that time, leaving at 14 was the law. I said I wanted to be a nurse, but my teacher said I would be a domestic. Well, she was both right and wrong.

In July 1944, at 13 and 11 months old, I left school. Most girls were excited but I liked school so I wasn't. A few of my friends had gone on to the grammar school but my mother wasn't agreeable for me to do that. I could have gone because I was good in school, but she said, "No, you've got to go to work." Unfortunately, you couldn't start training to be a nurse until you were 17. What I would have liked to have done before then was to work in a shop selling clothes and hats, but my mother had other ideas.

I left school on a Friday and the following Tuesday, she told me I had to go away to Weston-super-Mare and work in service looking after two children. There was no warning but I understand why. If I'd known, I would have run away to my grandmother's house because she was lovely and wouldn't have made me go. In those days, you had to do as you were told; you weren't allowed to say no, like I'm not doing it. I really didn't want to move away because I wasn't ready to leave home; I was very immature. But that's the way it was then.

My mother and our neighbour took me to the train station where we met a posh lady who was going to be my mistress. She got on the train with me at Cardiff and my mother left. I didn't have much with me, just a small case and two shillings and sixpence (12½p) in pocket money. The lady ate chocolate and offered me some, but I said, "No, thank you," because I felt sick.

We arrived at Weston-super-Mare where her husband, Doctor Stanley, met us. I never knew their Christian names. It started to rain, and when we arrived at the house, it seemed very big to me. It was a large detached place with a surgery in the basement. There were eight rooms plus a summer room. The storm got worse and there was thunder and lightning; inside, all the lights went out. The two children weren't there and I went to my room in pitch darkness. It was narrow with a door at one end and a window at the other, and there was just a bed and a chest of drawers. I wasn't given a uniform and I didn't have many clothes. The loneliness was awful, and all I could do was wait in my bed for nature to send me to sleep.

Early next morning, the lady called me to draw the curtains and lay the coal fire in the lounge. I pulled the curtains but I just did not know what to do with the fire. I was kneeling down and I felt like crying; eventually, the lady came in and she was shocked at the way the curtains were drawn. They were floor to ceiling curtains and she showed me how I should do it. I was very small and thin, and everything seemed big to me (I am 4ft 10ins now and was shorter then). The lady wasn't very happy with me because I hadn't laid the fire.

You see, my mother never put me to do anything at home as I had a brother and two sisters older than me. I did some shopping because I was good at adding up and making sure I had the right change. I was a good mixer so I had loads of friends to play with. I loved doing that and consequently I was not domesticated at all. At school, I learnt a bit about cooking and cleaning but never carried it through at home, and food was rationed anyway.

Although I thought I was going to be working as a nursemaid, I didn't do much work for the children. They were there because it was the school summer holidays. Nigel would have been about nine, and there was a little girl, Felicity, who was about five. I do remember them asking me to take the children down to their grandmother's house. It wasn't very far away and I was happy to do that, but I hardly ever got to work with the children. Their father was a doctor and their mother was a kind of society lady, she didn't work or anything and she wasn't very maternal.

The lady told me I was to call her 'Madam'. I had to work seven days a week, with just one half-day off in the week and every other Sunday as a half-day. All my duties were domestic: lots of cleaning and trying to cook. I just couldn't cook and I was frightened to death of doing it. The lady used to go off and have coffee with her friends and the doctor would be out on his rounds. She'd tell me to do the lunch and I couldn't do it. It really frightened me.

I continued to feel very lonely. I saw very little of the doctor and they both kept to themselves in the lounge. I had to stay in the kitchen where I had all my meals on my own. They would ring a bell from the dining room and I had to carry a tray and collect the dishes, then carry the dessert in. It was as if I had to keep separate from them, so I was on my own a lot. The lady saw me crying and said, "You are homesick, you will get over it." But I didn't, and I was so tired as I had such a lot of work to do.

On 3 August 1944, I had my fourteenth birthday but I don't remember it. I washed dishes a lot and cleaned the house, it seemed I was always alone and I was sad all the time. One day, I remembered the telephone number for our doctor at home and I knew that my mother went there some days to help out. So I phoned and the doctor's wife answered. She was a very nice lady and she called my mother to the telephone. I was crying, saying I didn't like it in Weston-super-Mare and I wanted to come home. But my mother told me I had to stay because I would soon settle, but I didn't.

I had my half-day on Wednesday when the lady gave me my wages. It was fifteen shillings and to be fair, this was not bad money then but I didn't care about money. I used to walk the streets on my own and the loneliness was unbearable. One day, the doctor and his wife went out and he told me to ring him only if someone had stomach pains, and not to let anyone in the house. It was a warm evening and I was ironing when the doorbell rang. On answering it, there was a dirty-looking man there begging to let him in. He was doing something in his pocket, which I did not understand but I closed the door quickly. He said he would come back the next day.

In the morning, I only saw the lady, not the doctor, and she was going out again, telling me to cook sausage and mash for dinner. I was very worried about the dirty-looking man coming back so I decided I must get away. After collecting my things, I left the house and found the train station by asking people the way. When I got home, my mother was out. My stepfather said, "I don't know what your mother's going to say," but I knew I was *not* going back. I was there for four long weeks and was very unhappy there; I might as well have been in prison! I was treated like a robot and I cried a lot.

Mother was shocked to see me but I immediately said I was not going back. She ordered me to phone the lady to say sorry for what I had done which reluctantly I did. I wasn't sorry, especially when she told me I had left her in the lurch.

Plans were now in progress by my mother to send me to Cardiff to a big house with a dance hall and billiard hall attached. It was closer to home but it made no difference. I didn't want to go, I couldn't eat but I had to go. I must say the family were very kind to me. I ate with them and in the evenings, I sat in the lounge with them too doing sewing.

There was a lot of very hard work during the day doing the washing the old-fashioned way with the mangle. There was a thick wooden stick for the washing boiler and I had to turn it vigorously for some minutes to clean the clothes. When the lady was satisfied, the clothes were wrung out and rinsed in clean, cold water several times, then mangled and pegged outside on the line. The lady taught me how to iron. There wasn't supposed to be any creases, no creases at all, which was very difficult to get right. There were no man-made fabrics then so it was a morning's job, usually on a Monday with ironing on a Tuesday. I really had to work hard there and I couldn't sleep because the music from the dance hall was so loud.

I was polishing the floor one day and I found two shillings and sixpence (12½p) under the carpet. I took it to the lady who said, "Good girl, you're very honest." Even though I still felt lonely and I missed my friends, it wasn't so bad and there was no cooking for me to do! The lady did some of it and her married daughter did some too. She was staying with her parents because her husband was still in the RAF. She had a little baby boy and I loved to take him out for a walk in the pram which was nice.

Then one Sunday afternoon, there was a knock at the front door and three of my friends were there. I was so excited and the lady said I could go out with them. We had a lovely afternoon with tea in a café but I had to say goodbye to them which was worse. I was very unsettled after that and their visit didn't do me any good at all.

The lady saw me crying and she said, "You're not happy, are you, Amy?"
I said, "No."
"Do you want to go home?"
I said, "Yes."
"Alright then, I'll write a note for your mother and I'll take you to the bus." She helped me to pack my little case and we parted on good terms. I lasted six months there before I went back home and I was now 14 and seven months old.

My mother was angry with me and said I had to work. I told her I was happy to work in a shop or in a factory as long as it was in the village where I was brought up. I had a lot of friends because I was always a good mixer and I missed them when I was sent away. In domestic service, I had learnt how to do housework and ironing so to please my mother, I did it at home to make her feel happy for me to stay. But she found me a job in a local shop instead.

I was very happy about this and asked, "Is it in a dress or shoe shop?"

She said, "No."

"Is it in a chemist's?"

"No."

"A veg shop?"

Finally, she said, "No, it's in a fish and chip shop."

I really didn't want to work in a fish and chip shop but my mother said it was either that or going back to Weston-super-Mare. I started there straight away and I was a bit nervous at first serving, but I grew to like it. There was lots of company and my friends and I met when I could. The wages were seven shillings a week, but I had good food and the lady and gentleman owners were very nice. It was very hard work and I had to scrub the shop after closing. I stayed there until a chance came for me to train as a nurse at Gloucester which I did. I was never lonely or sad again.

Looking back, I would have been much happier in a place where there were lots of other servants because I needed company of my own age. Although my experience in service was traumatic, I heard that some girls had a much worse time than me. When I got married and had my own children, I vowed that they would never have to leave home until they wanted to; they were 21 when they did.

My mother died in 2000 when she was 100 years old. I went to her funeral but will never go to her grave. Perhaps she thought she was doing her best for me, but I will never forget that lonely year as a servant.

When Amy turned seventeen, she trained as a nurse and enjoyed a long career in this profession. She married in 1952 and had two children.

Bibliography

Adams, Samuel and Sarah, *The Complete Servant* (Southover Press, 1989)

'An Engineer and His Wife', *The Ideal Servant-Saving House* (1918)

Anon, *Australia Invites the British Domestic Girl* (Development and Migration Commission, 1929)

Anon, *The Servants' Guide and Family Manual* (1831)

Anon, *The Servants' Practical Guide* (1880)

Ashford, Mary Ann, *The Life of a Licensed Victualler's Daughter, Written by Herself* (1844)

Banks, Elizabeth L., *Campaigns of Curiosity: Journalistic Adventures of an American Girl in London* (F. Tennyson Neely, 1894)

Barret-Ducrocq, Françoise, *Love in the Time of Victoria: Sexuality, Class and Gender in Nineteenth-Century London* (Verso, 1991)

Baylis, T. Henry, *The Rights, Duties and Relations of Domestic Servants, their Masters and Mistresses* (Sampson Low, Son & Co., 1857)

Beeton, Mrs Isabella, *The Book of Household Management* (S. O. Beeton Publishing, 1861)

Best, Geoffrey, *Mid-Victorian Britain 1851–1875* (Fontana Press, 1979)

Black, Clementina (ed.), *Married Women's Work: Being the Report of an Enquiry Undertaken by the Women's Industrial Council* (G. Bell & Sons, 1915)

Boase, Tessa, *The Housekeeper's Tale: The Women Who Really Ran the English Country House* (Aurum Press, 2014)

Booth, Charles (ed.), *Life and Labour of the People of London: Volume VIII Population Classified by Trades* (Macmillan & Co, 1896)

Bridgeman, Harriet and Drury, Elizabeth, *Victorian Household Hints* (Adam and Charles Black Publishers Ltd., 1981)

Burnett, John (ed.), *Useful Toil: Autobiographies of Working People from the 1820s to the 1920s* (Routledge, 1994)

Butler, C. V., *Domestic Service: An Enquiry by the Women's Industrial Council* (1916)

Caddy, Mrs Florence, *Household Organisation* (1877)

Canning, Audrey, 'Stephen, Jessie (1893–1979)', *Oxford Dictionary of National Biography* (Oxford University Press, 2004)

Casswell, J. D., *The Law of Domestic Servants: With a Chapter on the National Insurance Act, 1911* (Jordan & Sons, 1914)

Chinn, Carl, *They Worked All Their Lives: Women of the Urban Poor in England, 1880–1939* (Manchester University Press, 1988)

Collet, Clara, *Report on the Money Wages of Indoor Domestic Servants* (Board of Trade, 1899)

Crawshay, Rose Mary, *Domestic Service for Gentlewomen: A Record of Experience and Success* (1876)

Davey, Dolly, *A Sense of Adventure* (SE1 People's History Project, 1980)

Davies, Margaret Llewelyn (ed.), *Life As We Have Known It By Co-operative Working Women* (Virago Press, 1977)

Dawes, Frank Victor, *Not in Front of the Servants: A True Portrait of Upstairs, Downstairs Life* (Wayland, 1973)

Flanders, Judith, *The Victorian House* (Harper Collins, 2003)

Foley, Winifred, *A Child in the Forest* (British Broadcasting Corporation, 1974)

Hall, Edith, *Canary Girls and Stockpots* (Luton Workers' Educational Association, 1977)

Harrison, J. F. C., *Early Victorian Britain 1832–1851* (Fontana Press, 1988)

Harrison, J. F. C., *Late Victorian Britain 1875–1901* (Fontana Press, 1990)

Harrison, Rosina, *Rose: My Life in Service* (Cassell & Company Limited, 1975)

Higgs, Michelle, *Tracing Your Servant Ancestors* (Pen & Sword, 2012)

Horn, Pamela, *Life Below Stairs in the 20th Century* (Sutton Publishing, 2001)

Horn, Pamela, *My Ancestor was in Service: A Guide to Sources for Family Historians* (Society of Genealogists, 2009)

Horn, Pamela, *The Rise and Fall of the Victorian Servant* (Alan Sutton Publishing, 1986)

Horne, Eric, *What the Butler Winked At: Being the Life and Adventures of Eric Horne, Butler* (T. Werner Laurie, 1923)

Horsfield, Margaret, *Biting the Dust: The Joys of Housework* (Fourth Estate, 1997)

Jermy, Louise, *The Memories of a Working Woman* (1934)

Lethbridge, Lucy, *Servants: A Downstairs View of Twentieth-century Britain* (Bloomsbury, 2013)

Markham, Violet and Hancock, Florence, *Post-War Organisation of Private Domestic Employment* (1945)

Marshall, Dorothy, *The English Domestic Servant in History* (Historical Association, 1949)

May, Trevor, *The Victorian Domestic Servant* (Shire Publications, 2007)

Ministry of Labour, *Report to the Minister of Labour of the Committee Appointed to Inquire into the Present Conditions as to the Supply of Female Domestic Servants* (1923)

Ministry of Reconstruction, *Report of the Women's Advisory Committee on the Domestic Service Problem* (1919)

Mullins, Samuel and Griffiths, Gareth, *Cap and Apron: An Oral History of Domestic Service in the Shires, 1880–1950* (Leicestershire Museums, Art Galleries & Records Service, 1986)

Musson, Jeremy, *Up and Down Stairs: The History of the Country House Servant* (John Murray Publishers, 2009)

Panton, Jane Ellen, *From Kitchen to Garret* (Ward & Downey, 1888)

Phillips, R. Randall, *The Servantless House* (Country Life, 1920)

Powell, Margaret, *Below Stairs* (Pan Books, 1970)

Rennie, Jean, *Every Other Sunday: the Autobiography of a Kitchen-maid* (Arthur Barker, 1955)

Royston Pike, E., *Human Documents of the Age of the Forsytes* (George Allen & Unwin Ltd, 1969)

Royston Pike, E., *Human Documents of the Victorian Golden Age* (George Allen & Unwin Ltd, 1967)

Sambrook, Pamela, *Keeping Their Place: Domestic Service in the Country House* (Sutton Publishing, 2005)

Scadden, Rosemary, *No Job for a Little Girl: Voices from Domestic Service* (Gomer Press, 2013)

Schlüter, Auguste, *A Lady's Maid in Downing Street 1877–1890* (T Fisher Unwin Ltd., 1922)

Scott-Moncrieff, M. C., *Yes, Ma'am! Glimpses of Domestic Service 1901–1951* (Albyn Press Ltd, 1984)

Stanley, Elizabeth, *The Diaries of Hannah Cullwick: Victorian Maidservant* (Virago Press, 1984)

Stevenson, John, *British Society 1914–45* (Penguin Books, 1984)

Streatfeild, Noel (ed.), *The Day Before Yesterday: Firsthand Stories of Fifty Years Ago* (Collins, 1956)

Stuart Macrae, Mrs (ed.), *Cassell's Household Guide: A Complete Cyclopaedia of Domestic Economy* (The Waverley Book Company, 1911)

Turner, E. S., *What the Butler Saw: Two Hundred and Fifty Years of the Servant Problem* (Michael Joseph Ltd., 1962)

Waterson, Merlin, *The Servants' Hall: The Domestic History of a Country House*, (The National Trust, 1990)

Wise, Dorothy (ed.), *Diary of William Tayler, Footman 1837* (St. Marylebone Society, 1987)

Articles in Periodicals

Agnew, Lady, 'Ten Thousand A Year' in *Cornhill Magazine*, August 1901

Boucherett, Jessie, 'Legislative Restrictions on Women's Labour' in *Englishwoman's Review*, 1873

Colmore, G., 'Eight Hundred A Year' in *Cornhill Magazine*, June 1901

Delap, Lucy, 'Yes, ma'am: domestic workers and employment rights' in *History and Policy*, 3 September 2012

Earle, Mrs, 'Eighteen Hundred A Year' in *Cornhill Magazine*, July 1901

Faithfull, Emily, 'Domestic Service in England' in *The North American Review*, July 1891

Linton, Eliza Lynn, 'On the Side of the Maids' in *Cornhill Magazine*, 29, 1874 (pp. 298–307)

Linton, Eliza Lynn, 'On the Side of the Mistresses' in *Cornhill Magazine* 29, 1874 (pp. 459–68)

Marris, N. Murrell, 'Servant London' in *Living London*, 1902 (Vol. 2, pp. 351–357)

Martineau, Harriet, 'Modern Domestic Service' in *Edinburgh Review*, April 1862 (pp. 409–439)

Millin, George F., 'London Servants: High and Low' in *English Illustrated Magazine*, June 1894 (pp. 939–947)

Peel, Mrs C. S., 'Domestic Life in England Today' in *The North American Review*, February 1920

Robinson, John, 'A Butler's View of Men-Service' in *The Nineteenth Century: a Monthly Review*, June 1892

Todd, Selina, 'Poverty and Aspiration: Young Women's Entry to Employment in Inter-war England' in *Twentieth Century British History*, Vol. 15, No. 2, 2004

Periodicals and Newspapers

Berwickshire News and General Advertiser
Blackburn Standard
Cornhill Magazine
Country Life
Daily Gazette for Middlesbrough
Daily Mail
Edinburgh Review
English Illustrated Magazine
Englishwoman's Review
Gloucester Citizen
Hampshire Advertiser
Liverpool Echo
Liverpool Mercury
Living London
Northampton Mercury
Pall Mall Gazette
Punch
The Graphic
The Illustrated London News
The Lancet
The Morning Post
The North American Review
The Spectator
The Times
Western Mail

Index